THE MOUNTBATTENS

THE
MOUNTBATTENS
From Battenberg to Windsor

Douglas Liversidge

Arthur Barker Limited   London
A subsidiary of Weidenfeld (Publishers) Limited

Published in Great Britain by
Arthur Barker Limited
91 Clapham High Street
London SW4 7TA

ISBN 0 213 16686 0

Printed in Great Britain by
Butler & Tanner Ltd, Frome and London

Contents

Illustrations

Photographs are reproduced by gracious permission of Her Majesty the Queen (73), the Imperial War Museum (123b), Madame Hélène Cordet (141a and b and 145), London Express (151), Syndication International (151), and the Radio Times Hulton Picture Library.

Author's Note

For the purpose of brevity, the title of this book is merely *The Mountbattens*. Yet the text describes this unusual dynasty from the time it was first known as Battenberg – a name taken from ancient German aristocrats who, dying some centuries ago, gave their name to the little town of Battenberg.

The story of the Battenbergs-Mountbattens, the morganatic offshoot of the House of Hesse, reflects – due to a great extent to inter-marriage – a fair amount of the history of Britain and Europe over the last century and a quarter.

Two people who contributed to that story were Prince Louis of Battenberg and his wife, Princess Victoria, grand-daughter of the Queen-Empress Victoria. When their name was anglicized to Mountbatten in 1917, they became the first Marquess and Marchioness of Milford Haven, but to prevent confusion I refer to them as Prince Louis and Princess Victoria throughout the book.

THE MOUNTBATTENS

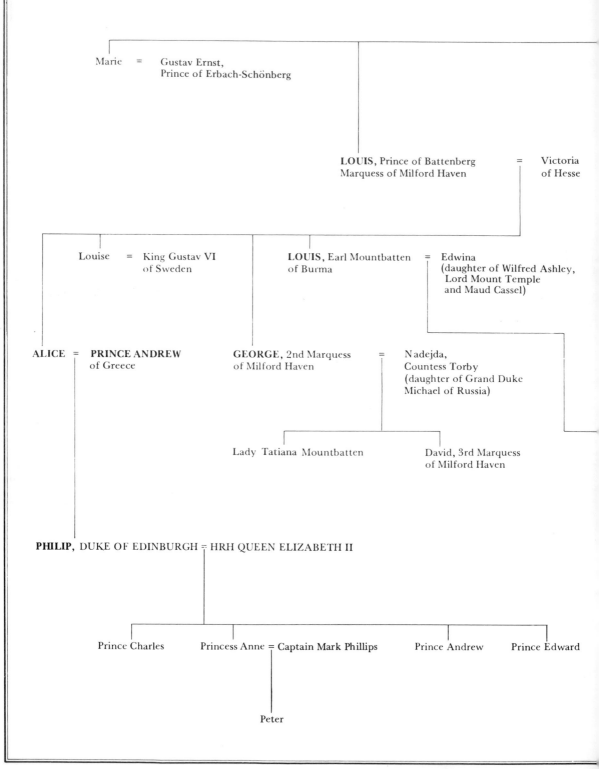

Marie = Gustav Ernst,
Prince of Erbach-Schönberg

LOUIS, Prince of Battenberg = Victoria
Marquess of Milford Haven   of Hesse

Louise = King Gustav VI   **LOUIS**, Earl Mountbatten = Edwina
of Sweden   of Burma   (daughter of Wilfred Ashley,
Lord Mount Temple
and Maud Cassel)

ALICE = **PRINCE ANDREW**   **GEORGE**, 2nd Marquess = Nadejda,
of Greece   of Milford Haven   Countess Torby
(daughter of Grand Duke
Michael of Russia)

Lady Tatiana Mountbatten   David, 3rd Marquess
of Milford Haven

PHILIP, DUKE OF EDINBURGH = HRH QUEEN ELIZABETH II

Prince Charles   Princess Anne = Captain Mark Phillips   Prince Andrew   Prince Edward

Peter

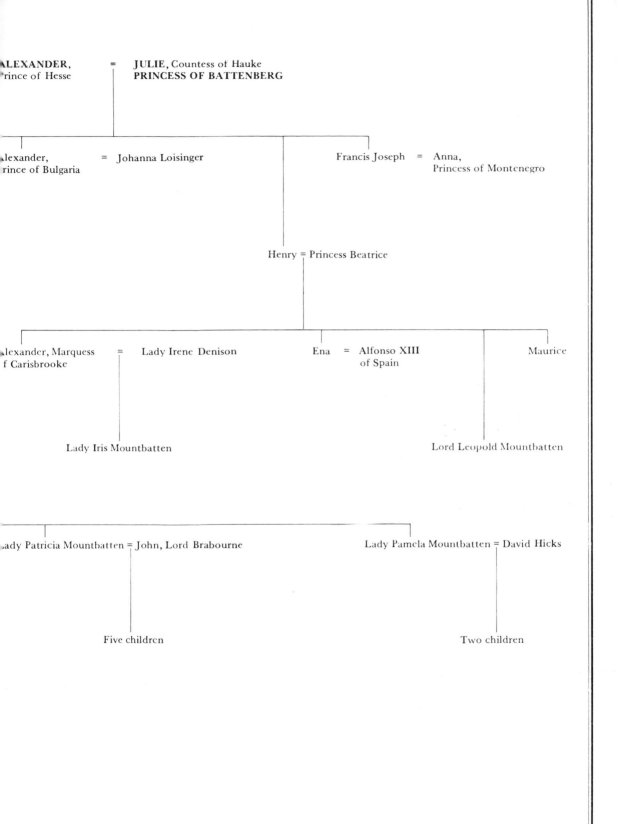

ALEXANDER, = JULIE, Countess of Hauke
Prince of Hesse PRINCESS OF BATTENBERG

Alexander, = Johanna Loisinger   Francis Joseph = Anna,
Prince of Bulgaria   Princess of Montenegro

Henry = Princess Beatrice

Alexander, Marquess = Lady Irene Denison   Ena = Alfonso XIII   Maurice
of Carisbrooke   of Spain

Lady Iris Mountbatten   Lord Leopold Mountbatten

Lady Patricia Mountbatten = John, Lord Brabourne   Lady Pamela Mountbatten = David Hicks

Five children   Two children

1

A Dynasty is Born

'THE witch-hunt of the First World War is one of the blackest pages in our history . . . and our family were not immune. Because he refused to abandon friends with German names, I was once asked whether it was true that my father drank the Kaiser's health after dinner.'

Thus wrote Violet Asquith of her father, then Prime Minister, who, in those early frenetic weeks of conflict, was foully abused for declining to intern the German maid who had served him for some thirty years. It was a symptom of the mass hysteria, the jingoism and the wild xenophobia which, kindled by the popular press, over-inflamed national passions. Hatred was paramount for things Germanic, symbolized in the maltreatment of dachshund dogs. Shops with German names had their windows broken, and even people with the slightest hint of an alien name were the butt of British spleen. Even Wagner's operas came under vicious attack.

If the Prime Minister himself could be falsely accused of nightly toasting the egotistical Kaiser at 10 Downing Street, there was bleak protection for anyone else against slanderous tongues. This grew starkly apparent to the handsome, bearded Prince Louis of Battenberg, who, as First Sea Lord, exercised supreme operational command of the Royal Navy. In his office at the Admiralty, or amid the magnificence of Mall House, his official residence in Admiralty Arch, this German princeling (whose wife, Princess Victoria, was the cousin of King George V) viewed with mounting alarm the anonymous letters with their humiliating accusations, and the rumours circulating in the clubs insinuating even Prince Louis's treachery.

Despite the fact that Louis's sons and nephews were already fighting for Britain, as the casualty lists lengthened public agitation heightened, demanding – through the newspapers led by *The Globe* – Prince Louis's dismissal. Unable to resist the destructive pressure, with a sense of profound sadness, he penned a letter of resignation.

Battenberg fortunes in the reign of Queen Victoria were very different. Attracted by the Battenberg princes, she had sanctioned the marriages of two of them into her family – acts which appalled the Hohenzollerns and other continental royalties, who expressed repugnance for Battenberg morganatic blood.

Victoria's grandson, King George V, on hearing of Prince Louis's resignation, could do nothing but remark: 'I feel deeply for him; there is no more loyal man in the country.'

Indeed, by 1917, anti-German prejudice would actually embroil the monarch himself. On Lloyd George's advice, he purged the royal house of its German princely titles. Thus the relatives of his consort, Queen Mary, replaced Teck with Cambridge, the Battenbergs anglicized their name to Mountbatten, and – doubtless to the matriarch's horror had she been aware – the beloved Prince Consort's dynasty of Saxe-Coburg and Gotha was now known as Windsor. On learning of this, the Kaiser directed that all performances of *The Merry Wives of Windsor* should henceforth be given under the title of *The Merry Wives of Saxe-Coburg and Gotha*.

But, in contrast, *Punch*, no doubt echoing public sentiment, published a drawing depicting the sovereign, wielding a besom, briskly sweeping into a heap crowns marked 'Made in Germany'. 'Good riddance', the caption claimed.

Thus the name Battenberg, which – dying out some centuries ago – had been resurrected for Countess Julie von Hauke, died once again.

If two particular young people had married, the Battenbergs would never have existed. When the twenty-one-year-old Alexander Nicolaievitch, heir to Tsar Nicholas I, came to Europe in search of a bride, he visited London, danced with Queen Victoria, taught her the steps of the mazurka and accompanied her to the theatre. For the Queen's reaction, one quotes her comment to her Prime Minister, Lord Melbourne: 'I think we are great friends already and get on very well; I like him exceedingly.' Her evident affection for the young man may well have alarmed the Coburgs, who wished Victoria to marry Prince Albert; however, their anxiety proved groundless, for the young Tsarevich encountered his future consort in the grand ducal palace in Darmstadt, Hesse – and rather fortuitously. After dinner, the fifteen-year-old Princess Marie mingled with the adults, and, despite her youth, the Romanoff heir was captivated by her beauty. The betrothal was probably not so surprising, for Elizabeth, the Dowager-Empress of Russia, widow of the late Tsar Alexander I (who had been succeeded by his brother Nicholas), was the sister of Marie's late mother, the Grand Duchess Wilhelmina, and had long cherished the possibility of a union between the Tsarevich and her niece.

Marie's delicate health induced her father, the Grand Duke Louis II, to delay the engagement until 16 April 1840, when the Tsarevich – Sasha, as he was known by his family and intimates – presented Marie with a diamond bracelet from the Russian crown treasures. To her embarrassment, she lost it the same day, retrieving it only after a gardener's daughter came across it by chance. Invested with the pomp and ritual of the Russian Orthodox Church, the wedding ceremony was solemnized in St Petersburg on 28 April 1841.

Prince Alexander of Hesse, now eighteen, and a year older than Princess Marie, accompanied his sister to the Imperial Court – a step which led to a notorious mid-nineteenth-century romance; unpardonably, Alexander fell in love with his sister's lady-in-waiting, Julie von Hauke, a young countess condescendingly referred to at

Court as 'that poor, sweet Polish girl'. It was a misalliance, a gross contravention of the social standards set by Europe's hierarchy in those days. But from it emerged a unique family – the Battenberg, later Mountbatten, line.

For Marie, life in Russia imposed an acute strain. Her autocratic mother-in-law, Prussian by birth, scarcely veiled her dislike for the House of Hesse, and the winter snows and the harsh winds from the swamps undermined her health. There were also the malicious tongues; soon they were reviving a rumour that had long been whispered in European courts. Focusing on the gap between the ages of Alexander and Marie and their older brothers, the gossips hinted that the young children were the offspring of a clandestine liaison between the Grand Duchess of Hesse and her Chamberlain, Baron Augustus von Grancy. No one, however, could prove the validity of this insinuation, and the Tsar contemptuously remarked: 'We can only hope to be the sons of our fathers whose proud name we bear, but who on earth can prove it?' He therefore ordered the gossiping to stop.

Marie's brother, however, was much happier there. A godson of the late Tsar, who had commissioned him as a second lieutenant in the Russian army at his christening, Alexander revelled in the excitement of the Imperial Court, even if the Tsarina did not conceal her repugnance for his ancestry. The more agreeable Tsar, however, re-christened the Borrisoglebosky 17th Lancers after Alexander and appointed him their colonel-in-chief.

Like other young blades at Court, Alexander – intelligent, handsome and physically strong – had a weakness for beautiful women. Unfortunately he lost his heart to the Tsar's own daughter, the Grand Duchess Olga, whose hand in marriage had been promised to the heir of the King of Württemberg. But war was some antidote to a bruised heart. Promoted to brigadier-general, he joined an army raised to crush a rebellion in the Caucasus, where Shamyl, the tribal leader, now legendary throughout Europe, was trying to rid his people of tsarist power.

On 6 April 1845, Alexander entered in his diary this plaintive note: 'I do not know whether Olly really loves me. She was little affected when I said good-bye. All she gave me as a farewell was to read every day the 19th Psalm as a memento of her.'

Frightful bloodshed and shocking brutality characterized the war, the prisoners on either side being ruthlessly tortured. Alexander, however, was destined for a more unusual fate if captured. Writing to his sister and the Tsarevich, he revealed: 'We are terribly depressed, our position is perilous ... we cannot return the way we came, and before us lie dark forests full of fanatical foes.' As for himself, 'according to reports of prisoners we have taken, Shamyl's wife has asked her husband to be given the German prince (me) when he is captured.' But Alexander retained his freedom and distinguished himself in fierce fighting. Today, in the care of his descendant, Earl Mountbatten, are Alexander's trophies of war: Shamyl's Koran and papers together with the Prince's pistols.

3

During six months 'of well-deserved leave', Alexander gave a glimpse of that rebellious, independent spirit without which there would have been no Battenberg, or Mountbatten, line. In defiance of the unbending social code of his time, writing to his sister from Vienna, he confided:

It seems that one should marry to please oneself and not to please other people. I grieve for Olly and I am not at all happy about your suggestions about Vivi [Louise of Mecklenburg-Schwerin]. I am not at all disposed to tie myself down at the age of twenty and three. If I marry her, I shall have to stay in Darmstadt with the prospect of doing nothing all the rest of my life or in St Petersburg where I cannot live a married life at all without money. So you will not be surprised if I avoid the trap that is set for me so openly.

Again in Russia, the Prince yielded to the temptations of gambling, drinking and women – dissolution on a scale which displeased the Tsar. The money needed for these extravagances seems to have been Alexander's main anxiety. He thus had recourse to money-lenders, before resorting to more devious means, following a widespread practice at Court; for many grew rich from money derived from clandestine sources or accepted gifts for the occasional discreet service. At times some even sold Russian state secrets to European powers. Alexander at least preferred more commendable dealings with the Rothschilds.

Mayer Amschel Rothschild and his sons had long shed their early poverty in Jew Street in the Frankfurt ghetto. Now, from their mansions in London, Paris and other strategic centres, their ramifications penetrated deep into Europe's seats of power. Their shadow fell on many courts and governments of which not a few had need to show gratitude. Typical was the Elector of Hesse-Cassel who, fleeing in 1806 before the all-conquering Bonaparte, relied on old Mayer Amschel to safeguard his wealth. Indeed, the Rothschild link with the Grand Dukes of Hesse extended over many years.

Not unnaturally, the Rothschilds now regarded Alexander as the perfect device with which to complete their financial empire – a branch in St Petersburg. Thus the second Mayer Amschel sent a skilful negotiator, Moses Davidson, to Russia to offer Alexander a lucrative annuity if he would induce the Tsar to accept credits to finance the state budgets and the new railways. But Steiglitz, the German bankers, had monopolized the major financial dealings in Russia for many years, and the Tsar's advisers were determined that they should continue. Their most potent weapon concerned the Russian attitude to Jews, who were prohibited by law from permanent residence; moreover, no Jewish concern could employ more than five clerks. Arousing hostility at Court, Prince Alexander's overtures proved abortive. St Petersburg would continue to be the only prominent European centre to ban the Rothschilds. They would harbour resentment.

For a while, Prince Alexander was equally unsuccessful in affairs of the heart. At a ball in January 1848, one Countess Shuvalov warned him to cease paying attention to

Prince Alexander of Hesse with his wife, formerly Julie von Hauke, who was eventually created a Princess of Battenberg. They founded the Battenberg (or Mountbatten) dynasty – the morganatic line of the House of Hesse.

Alexander's cousin, the Emperor Francis Joseph of Austria with his wife. He gave Alexander military service after his banishment from Russia, and for some years Alexander served the Austrian monarchy as a military commander and on occasions as a diplomat.

her daughter Sophie, her message being conveyed by one of his sister's ladies-in-waiting – Julie von Hauke. The annoyance of the Countess Shuvalov would create history, for with Prince Alexander her messenger would establish the House of Battenberg, later Mountbatten.

Julie was the orphan daughter of a Russian general killed during the Polish revolution of 1831. In her memoirs years later, her daughter Marie explained that Julie's Polish

extraction always had about it a halo of romance. Nothing interested me more than to learn something about her relatives, but she never spoke of them herself. As the youngest of her family, brought up in St Petersburg, she had less of the Polish element about her than the rest. Now and then she would mention a member of the Hauke family, and the events of which she told were always shadowed by the tragedy of her nation, for not only her father but other family members too had died violent deaths.

Julie's great-grandfather had, it appears, been a tradesman in Mainz, and his son Johann gained some prominence: attendance at the Latin school secured him a clerkship in the State Office of the King of Saxony (who was then also King of Poland) before graduating as secretary to the Governor of Warsaw. When Poland was apportioned to Russia and Prussia, Johann Hawke – who decided on the more aristocratic 'Hauke' – stayed in Warsaw in Russian employ, marrying the daughter of the pastor of Sassenheim, Marie Salome Schweppenhauser.

Of their seven children, Moritz, the eldest, received a command in the Tsar's army. Hauke allegiance, however, was flexible. When Poland retrieved independence through Napoleon, he enlisted in the Polish Legion and fought under Bonaparte's flag. And when Napoleon's military fortunes waned, he returned to Poland, again switching allegiance, to take command of a brigade of Tsar Alexander's army. In 1820 he rose to more rarefied heights as Minister of War in the Russian-controlled satellite government of Poland. Four years later Moritz Hauke married Sophie Lafontaine, daughter of a French doctor who, with his Hungarian wife, lived at Biberach-on-the-Riss near Lake Constance in Württemberg. Moritz was fifteen years older than his wife, who bore him three children. It was a strange coincidence that, as War Minister, he and his family resided at the Palais Brühl where his father had served the Saxon governor in a less august role.

Promoting Moritz Hauke to the rank of general in 1829, Tsar Nicholas added the title of count. But Moritz, the loyal pawn, and his title, would be short-lived; within a year – in November – he was killed by revolutionaries while trying to protect the Governor-General, the Tsar's brother, the Grand Duke Constantine. For Countess Sophie Hauke, the hacking down of her husband proved devastating: within a year she was dead of a broken heart, and Tsar Nicholas instructed that her orphans should be reared as wards at Court.

Julie von Hauke was twenty-three years old when, in 1848, she met Alexander of

6

Hesse at the Russian Court. Little more than five feet tall, she had, according to her daughter's memoirs,

rather a thickset figure, but her large soft brown eyes, her lovely little mouth and her hands were wonderfully pretty; even when she was old, the latter were a poem in colour and form. Her voice also had great charm, and her delightful, trilling laugh ... showed all her pretty teeth ... Mamma spoke pure and fluent German ... She read a great deal of German; the classics for preference. She also read, with equal fluency, Dante in Italian and Shakespeare in English; while Russian, Polish and French were to her mother-tongues.

A painting of Countess Julie depicts her with dark brown hair parted in the middle and adorned with looped pearls. The long straight nose infuses her features with that determination and strength which became paramount in later years; it became a distinctive feature in successive generations of Battenbergs to the present day.

Judging Prince Alexander of Hesse on his behaviour, his meeting with Julie did not seem to generate a sudden romance. Indeed, the Prince persisted in meeting Sophie Shuvalov secretly – and, curiously, with Julie's aid as trusted confidante. The liaison, however, ended abruptly. When the Countess Shuvalov discovered the truth, she carried out her threat and complained to the Tsar. Nicholas firmly ordered Alexander to end the affair or quit the Court, recommending his marriage to his niece, the Grand Duchess Catherine, daughter of his brother Michael. The possibility of a Balkan throne was also dangled before him.

If Alexander had adhered to the Tsar's wishes, the Battenbergs would never have originated. But circumstances were taking their course. On 15 July 1848 – his twenty-fifth birthday among the love-notes that Prince Alexander received was one from Countess Julie. 'I really did not notice that the girl was in love with me,' wrote the Prince. Countess Julie became Alexander's mistress, an intimacy of which the Tsar remained ignorant until, during the autumn of 1849, opening a door in the Tsarevna's suite, he noticed his ward and the Prince in a passionate embrace. Threatening to despatch Alexander to a Siberian garrison, the enraged Tsar placed him under the discipline of the Grand Duke Michael, commander-in-chief of the Imperial Guard. It resulted in intolerable persecution, and in August 1850 the Tsar granted Alexander's request to take indefinite leave.

After calling at Darmstadt – where his elder brother, as Louis III, now occupied the grand ducal throne – Alexander stayed in Paris before gaining his first experience of London. The Prince was genuinely surprised by 'the liberal ways of life in London' – an impression which (as in the case of his descendants) would endear Britain to him. After visiting the offices of *The Times*, he wrote to his sister Marie in Russia: 'It is utterly amazing how the journalists can write quite freely about the Royal Family, even about the private lives of Queen Victoria and her Consort in a newspaper which is being read by everybody.'

On his return to Russia in 1851, Prince Alexander met with a frigidity which

7

dispirited him. The climax was reached when the Grand Duke Michael, conspiring to have him banned from the Imperial Court, untruthfully alleged that the Prince's behaviour had 'absolutely demoralized the Officer Corps'. Alexander concluded that he must leave his adopted country.

At this stage it is not possible to gauge the true relationship between Alexander and Julie. In the previous year, when the betrothal of Sophie Shuvalov and Prince Brobrinsky had been announced, Prince Alexander had written dejectedly in his diary: 'I cannot bear the idea of Sophie belonging to someone else.' But now, confiding in Julie that he proposed to quit St Petersburg, he agreed to take her with him. Was, therefore, the Battenberg line merely the result of an impulsive action? Whatever the explanation, the outcome of their engagement was explosive. Because Countess Julie was a ward of the Crown, Alexander required the Tsar's consent to the marriage. The Prince must have expected refusal; he was breaking an inflexible code by wishing to marry outside his caste. One day Alexander's sister would be crowned Empress of All the Russias, and to the Court it was unthinkable that her sister-in-law should be her former lady-in-waiting. The objection went even deeper than that. It was an age in which one's actions were influenced greatly by who one was, and that depended solely on family. On matters of marriage, it was the rigid rule among royalty to accept no one outside their own class. A misalliance must be ruthlessly ostracized. Although years later circumstances would change her mind, Queen Victoria summarized the prevailing attitude with the remark: 'A morganatic marriage is something we would never wish to discuss.'

Marie's fears that the marriage might undermine her status at Court went unheeded. So, too, did the words of the Grand Duke Louis in Darmstadt, who advised his brother to marry 'one of the girls of that big litter of Catherine the Great'. Sasha advised that to wed without the Tsar's consent would mean banishment from Russia – a dire warning confirmed by an incensed Tsar some weeks later. The Prince was equally adamant. On 4 October 1851 Alexander and Julie, travelling separately until they reached Warsaw, fled from the Court. They continued to Breslau in Prussian Silesia, where a priest married them on 28 October. When the Tsar learned of this, Alexander was promptly cashiered from the Imperial Guard.

At the age of twenty-eight, Prince Alexander of Hesse was divested of military rank and money. Just as irksome and demanding was the barbed question of Julie's status, for, being of inferior rank, she could not be accepted as a princess of Hesse. This was a family knot which Louis III asked his disgruntled Chief Minister, Karl von Dalwigk, to unravel, when he summoned him on the cheerless night of 3 November 1851. It was raining hard as the minister's carriage rumbled into the Parade Platz, then along the drive to the sixteenth-century palace. Sitting before the library fire and tortured by gout, Louis testily asked his minister how they could regularize a ridiculous marriage which had annoyed so many – even the British Queen. Explaining the constitutional aspect, Dalwigk pointed out that Prince Alexander would retain his title and rank, and

Marie, Prince Alexander's sister, who married the heir to the Russian throne. Alexander grew in political stature when Marie's husband became Tsar Alexander II.

The Grand Duke Louis III of Hesse and the Rhine, Alexander's brother, who first elevated Julie to Countess of Battenberg – the name of a knightly family who had died out centuries earlier.

his wife could be raised to the dignity of a countess of the Grand Duchy of Hesse-Darmstadt and the Rhine. Any children of the marriage would bear the mother's name and would have no right to princely titles.

'But what name?' asked Louis. At first Dalwigk suggested 'Kellerberg': there was a castle of that name dating from the fifteenth century; but Louis thought it unsuitable. Dalwigk now mentioned a little town near Wiesbaden named after an ancient knightly family which had participated in the Crusades. Since the family had died out in the fourteenth century, the title was defunct, but it could be revived. 'They were the Counts von Battenberg, Your Highness,' said Dalwigk. 'They had a fine castle overlooking the River Eder at Battenberg. The round tower and bastions still stand on the eastern heights of the Westerwald.'

The decree announcing Julie's Battenberg title was issued two days later. Dalwigk also notified Alexander that, for political reasons, his presence in Darmstadt would create no small embarrassment. And so the Prince and his newly-acquired wife travelled to Geneva, living in a small private hotel until sister Marie and brother Louis supplied the means to rent a villa. It was there that their first child, Marie, was born. Her arrival seemed to betoken greater prosperity. Alexander's young cousin, the Emperor Francis Joseph of Austria, offered military service, and through the mediation of Sasha, the Tsar placed Alexander on the retired list as a major-general.

In the following October, Francis Joseph appointed Alexander garrison commander at Graz. Military duties were not onerous, and to counter tedium Alexander and Julie, together with certain local dignitaries, dabbled in occultism at the castle in Graz. Louis, their eldest son, was born there on 24 May 1854. One day he would be the eminent but controversial First Sea Lord at the British Admiralty, father of Earl Mountbatten of Burma and grandfather of Prince Philip, Duke of Edinburgh.

For the next eight years Prince Alexander served the Austrian monarchy with distinction, commanding a division of the army of occupation at Verona in northern Italy, where another son, Alexander (nicknamed 'Sandro' by the family) was born in 1857, to be followed the next year by a third, Henry (Liko), when he was transferred to Milan. Returning to Darmstadt at intervals, the family led a nomadic life, yet in grandiose style. Typical was their spacious residence, Casa Somailow, in Milan. In later life Marie recalled that in the garden she and her brothers spent many blissful hours,

particularly as someone had given us two black sheep, which were harnessed to a little carriage. There were splendid rooms in the house: a ballroom with sky-blue silk furnishings and a profusion of gold, and a dining-room, whose ceilings and walls were painted with chubby-cheeked children, carrying in their hands fruit and vegetables, wild-fowl and game. Our night-nursery was a very large, lofty room; it had a smooth green carpet which looked like a meadow, and on the ceiling was a crowd of gods and goddesses.

The philandering days were over. Prince Alexander was now a devoted husband and father. In a little dark private room Marie's parents would sit after dinner.

Papa sat smoking by the fire and used to take Louis and me on his knee, letting us ride and fall off. He used to give us, too, the straws which were stuck through his long Virginia cigars, and then would read his newspaper quite through to the end. Day after day we waited patiently until he had finished, and then came the great moment when he threw the paper tightly folded on to the flames. Day after day, with unfailing delight and attention, we knelt in front of the fireplace watching the burning paper crinkle up and the strange shapes it took, till at last it all sank together in a heap of ashes... we were very seldom alone with our parents. Commonly one or other of the aides was present.

For a while domestic peace was destroyed. In 1858 Prince Alexander witnessed the riots in Italy and the growth of the secret societies of Garibaldi, and in the following year he commanded an Austrian infantry division in the brief war against a resurgent Italy aided by the French. Countess Julie's letters to her sister Sophie disclosed that every day fresh troops were arriving, and Alexander decided to send his wife and family back to Hesse. Julie was reluctant to travel at that time of year, largely because of the difficulties of taking four young children such a long way. She therefore decided to wait until April.

Louis had developed mumps and was carried from his bed to the carriage on the day of departure. Everyone wept at being separated from Prince Alexander. The whole household was in disorder – a chaotic scene of trunks, excitement and lamentation. The rain poured incessantly, and it was nightfall before the party reached an inn. Writing again on 12 May, Julie explained: 'If I could play the Emperor of the French some kind of evil trick, I believe I should be delighted ... My journey was beyond everything painful, melancholy and wearisome. I reached Darmstadt only on the tenth day. It was dreadful – the poor children arrived quite exhausted.'

Alexander fought in two fierce battles – Magenta and Solferino – and at the latter led a battalion of Imperial Guards in a bayonet charge and prevented a rout.

After the clamour of battle, Julie informed her sister that her husband had been entrusted with a diplomatic mission; Napoleon III had consented to come to terms with the Austrians, by the Treaty of Villafranca. 'The day before the meeting in Villafranca,' she wrote, 'he was sent by the Emperor of Austria with a letter in his own hand to Louis Napoleon, with verbal instructions also, and *carte blanche*. My husband ... promised me some very interesting details about this mission, of which the result was a most interesting exchange of letters between him and Napoleon. They had already met at Plombières and Stuttgart.'

Prince Alexander had grown in political stature after his banishment from Russia – especially when Sacha succeeded to the tsarist throne as Alexander II. Indeed, he was the confidant of kings and sometimes the intermediary in the political machinations of Russia, Austria and France. For these subtle assignments he had chosen the perfect wife, for Countess Julie possessed the ideal temperament for political intrigue. She never neglected her husband's ambitions, nor could her loyalty be questioned. Writing to her sister from Hesse during the Italian campaign, she confided: 'If it had not been for the children, I would never have left Italy. There I was at least nearer ... and could nurse him in the event of any misfortune – the great distance which separates me from my loved one horrifies me! . . . I often think of going back alone.'

But how pronounced were her maternal instincts? In her memoirs, Julie's eldest child Marie revealed that, certainly up to the time the family moved to Milan, she did not remember much about her parents in those years.

We children [she wrote] lived entirely to ourselves with Adèle [Bassing] and our maid, who at first was old Evi, and later a Swiss girl named Hortense, and then Hariet, an Englishwoman. We saw papa nearly always in uniform and on horseback ... He was, and remained, the sunshine of our lives, not only in childhood but in later life ... Of mamma we always stood a little in awe, because she was strict and made us speak French with her; she probably loved us all alike, but it was her habit to be always most tender with the youngest child, and I remember how we elder ones would sometimes comment upon this among ourselves. Praise from her always made a great impression on us.

Marie further added that Adèle soon became 'next to my father, the one I loved best of all about me. Her influence gradually extended itself to all my brothers ... to her I owe almost everything that made in the days of my youth for the training of my heart and intellect.'

Probably Marie later changed her views, for elsewhere she relates that Countess Julie – a Russian Pole and a Catholic (although she later became a Protestant) – 'had only a good and fostering influence on the German upbringing of her family, and on the Protestant spirit of the house, for she devoted herself entirely to the dawning life of her children'.

For years Countess Julie patiently endured humiliation due to her inferior rank, such as the occasion in November 1856 when the Emperor Francis Joseph and the Empress Elizabeth visited Verona. Irritated by Prince Alexander's Russian sympathies, the Emperor foolishly instructed that the Countess of Battenberg should be placed with 'the ladies with lower birth', while her husband stood elsewhere as a prince. He went further: Julie was deliberately ignored as she curtsied. Alexander therefore rejoiced when his brother Louis III elevated Julie to the rank of Princess of Battenberg at Christmas 1858, thereby entitling her children and descendants to be known as princes and princesses of the House of Battenberg with the embellishment 'Durchlaucht', 'Serene Highness'.

Three years later, after Solferino, a grateful Austrian Emperor promoted Alexander to lieutenant-general and awarded him the rare Order of Maria Theresa. The same year witnessed his transfer to Padua and the birth of Francis Joseph, his youngest son. From Hesse the entire household moved over the Alps to their new Italian home – the Casa Arenberg, a magnificent mansion with a paved court in which stood a massive statue of Hercules. Again, it is from Marie's memoirs that one derives a vivid impression of these family travels. She wrote: 'I can see us on the heights of the Splügen, distributed in several carriages; papa snowballed us; then we went serpenting downwards.' At each curve they waved to the heavily-laden vehicle upon which, behind a heap of assorted trunks, a married couple, the Illerts, sat – the faithful companions of their nomadic life.

Eventually the wanderings ceased. During the next year, Prince Alexander retired and settled with his family in Hesse. In the winter the Battenbergs resided in the Alexander Palace, an attractive rococo mansion on the Luisenplatz in Darmstadt (in modern times converted for use as the central post office). The summer months were spent near the village of Jugenheim at twin-towered Heiligenberg, a castle in a wooded valley flanked by pine-clad mountains.

As far as one can trace, very few of Princess Julie's Polish relatives ever visited Heiligenberg. First came Alexander von Hauke, Julie's twenty-year-old nephew, a patriot exiled by the Tsar. Dedicated to liberating Poland from Russian oppression, after studying at Heidelberg University, he returned to his native country in 1863, took part in the anti-tsarist revolution and died for his country. His father, yet another Alexander, visited Heiligenberg two years later. Another relative, the revolutionary Count Joseph von Hauke, was rarely mentioned by the Battenbergs. Discarding his family's name, he preferred to be called 'Boszak' (Barefoot) and died in 1867 fighting in support of Garibaldi at the Battle of Giacomo. Many years later, Princess Marie of Battenberg recalled that by chance, in Neuchâtel, she met a sympathetic young woman who introduced herself as the daughter of Joseph von Hauke. 'From her I heard so much that was noble and impressive about her father that I have since then deeply regretted never having seen him,' she wrote.

In the 1860s, an event occurred which not only enhanced the House of Hesse but in due course bound the Battenbergs inseparably with the royal family in Britain. Prince Alexander's nephew, Prince Louis of Hesse, who would succeed the childless Louis III as Grand Duke, was betrothed to Princess Alice, the second daughter of Queen Victoria. The English connection, it is said, prompted Alexander to consider journeying to England, to renew his contact with the Rothschilds and enter business, but at the Tsar's request he remained in Germany. Bismarck, Prussia's 'Iron Chancellor', who was scheming for German unification and looked upon Austria as an obstruction, was trying to establish stronger links between Prussia and Russia. The Tsar asked Alexander to acquaint him of any developments that transpired.

Bismarck would soon obtrude further into Prince Alexander's life and treat the Battenbergs with suspicion. When, for instance, King Otto fled from revolution in Greece, Count Rechberg, the Austrian Foreign Minister, approached Alexander, seeking his candidature for the vacant throne. The offer was supported by the Tsar, Napoleon III and the British Government, but Bismarck vetoed it because of Alexander's connections with Austria and Russia. If Alexander had worn the Greek crown, Battenberg history would definitely have taken a different course.

This was the second throne that had eluded Alexander. Sasha, his brother-in-law,

13

had assured him in 1857 that he would 'look for a crown' for him, 'perhaps as the ruler of a new Rumania'. In 1870, Napoleon III submitted Alexander's candidature for the Spanish throne, but the Tsar and the Austrian and British Governments declined to collaborate with France against Bismarck. Nothing ever matured, but three decades hence Alexander would see his namesake son mount the throne of neighbouring Bulgaria.

Time would demonstrate how an event in Britain would lead to a more secure and durable future for the Battenbergs. Queen Victoria welcomed Prince Alexander to her Court. Whether or not it was the matriarch's sympathetic gesture because the British Government had ceded to Bismarck, is immaterial. The fact is that on 5 April 1863 Alexander attended the christening at Windsor Castle of Victoria, the daughter of his nephew Louis and Princess Alice, who would one day marry Prince Louis, his son. As for Prince Alexander himself, he personally impressed the Queen. Writing to her daughter, the Crown Princess of Prussia, on 29 April 1863, Victoria commented: 'I am much struck by Prince Alexander of Hesse. I think him very clever and agreeable. He was talking to us yesterday evening of the Peace of Villa Franca and I thought old times were returned, and Papa must be listening to it or that I must tell it him all again! How it would have interested him for he was so unhappy about all that.'

Beginning in the reign of Queen Victoria, a Battenberg, or Mountbatten, would in varying degrees contribute to the story of the British Crown, from the time when Alexander's son Henry, or 'Liko', married the Queen's youngest daughter Beatrice and came to enjoy the matriarch's closest confidence as companion and adviser. Between Prince Alexander and the Prince of Wales (the future Edward VII) there would also develop a rapport. Alexander described Victoria's heir as 'a funny little man. His features are not bad; he is a male edition of his sister Alice, but he is so broad for his height that he looks shorter than his wife.'

Alexander created a pattern to be followed by his descendants. In London, he had meetings with Lord Palmerston, the Prime Minister, and Lord John Russell, his Foreign Secretary, and Alexander – always loyal to the Tsar – wrote to Russia explaining that the British statesmen 'treated me as a colleague; they are well informed through their secret agents about some of the negotiations I have conducted with Napoleon and Francis Joseph.'

Having retired from regular army life, Prince Alexander devoted more time to the future of his children. At their country residence, the Battenberg offspring and their parents – whom the German Emperor hailed as the most handsome family in Europe – welcomed their contemporaries from the Courts of St Petersburg, London and Berlin. Heiligenberg was the rendezvous of Europe's houses of power. The Battenberg–Mountbatten relationship with Europe's other royal dynasties should not be underestimated. Princess Ena of Battenberg, for instance, would become the Queen of Spain, and Princess Louise Mountbatten would identify her family with the royal house of Sweden. But it was the link by marriage to Queen Victoria's descendants that stabilized and nurtured their status in modern times. Prince Louis of Battenberg, for example, married a grand-daughter of the Queen-Empress, his brother Henry her youngest daughter. Just as Prince Henry had been the confidant and adviser of Queen Victoria, so Prince Louis was an intimate of Edward VII and George V. His son, Earl Mountbatten of Burma, would enjoy the closest friendship with Edward VIII and George VI. But Prince Louis's grandson, Philip Mountbatten, would transcend all by becoming the consort of the British Queen – the First Gentleman of the Realm.

2

An Intricate Cousinhood

FOR two years, during the rebuilding of the Alexander Palace, the Battenbergs lived at the Old Palace in Darmstadt, the setting of Prince Alexander's childhood. Alexander occupied the ground-floor apartments on the right side of the main entrance. Julie and the children were allotted rooms on the first floor and a wing overlooking the Wilhelmstrasse. It was an environment of old-world opulence, with massive mirrors reaching down to costly carpets or glistening parquet. Ancestral portraits linked the present with the past. From their vantage-point, the children looked down on 'plain, comfortable houses, and pretty shop windows'.

As his later career would testify, Louis was the most competent and talented of the young Battenbergs. Kind and congenial by nature, he learned swiftly and easily, and all his skills had 'fallen into his lap in the same measure', wrote his sister Marie. His gift for languages was impressive and, when he was only four years old, there were incipient signs of his future skill as an artist. Julie and Alexander transmitted their penchant for the arts to their children, in a taste for painting and the theatre, the ballet and the opera, and Louis's love of music – no doubt encouraged by Prince Alexander, an accomplished pianist – was pronounced. Indeed, the music academy of Professor Phillip Schmidt, Alexander's lifelong friend, created much of the childhood atmosphere of the Battenberg offspring. All participated in the general instruction and the collective performances at the annual examination-concert, for which eight or ten pianos were used. When at Heiligenberg, Alexander and his family, accompanied by a servant carrying a lantern on dark nights, would sometimes walk to the Villa Pauer in Jugenheim, where Alexander played duets with Ernest Pauer, the distinguished concert pianist.

Julie, however, could not tolerate the music of Wagner. Once attending a performance of *The Valkyrie* on her own, she afterwards commented: 'It was intolerable, the pitch-dark cottage and the men dressed up as animals. But when Bär [the tenor] began to climb trees like a monkey, I left the box!' For years Alexander shared his wife's sentiments, yet, ironically, the last music he would ever hear would be *Parsifal*, in Bayreuth, a month before his death. Wagner did in fact visit Darmstadt at the age of seventy; he probably had aspirations to found his festival theatre there. Whatever his motive, he was discouraged; Prince Alexander, then patron of the theatre, offered bleak

16

encouragement, and the Grand Duke, rather horrified, cried: 'God forbid! I should have to give *Gotha Almanach* dinners the whole summer.'

On Sundays he kept a generous table. It was a ritual: the four o'clock family dinner, when it was imperative for everyone – including the Battenbergs – to attend in evening dress. The guests, some still lethargic through having eaten and drunk so recently, were summoned for tea at eight o'clock.

Princess Alice of Hesse thought the custom uncivilized and eventually absented herself, much to the Grand Duke's annoyance. Instead, she had lunch served at her own residence at two o'clock, with tea at the normal English time. Alice did not take too easily to her Hessian environment.

She was a foreigner, came from distant England [explained Princess Marie years later] and ... did not fit in at all with the Darmstadt connections. I often felt sorry for her, she was so kind and so congenial to us, more so than our Hesse relations, and in a different way. To these last, my mother, likewise, notwithstanding all their love and kindness, always remained a foreigner.

In our circle but little was known, in those days, of England and English customs; of its luxury and practical, solid enjoyment of life; and it was a long while before the really very great difference between the modest little house in Darmstadt and the castle at Windsor was appreciated.

Alice no doubt received the sympathy of her sister Vicky, the Crown Princess of Prussia, whose early married life was similarly marred by the hostility of her mother-in-law. What nauseated Alice most of all was the Grand Duke himself. The immense Louis III – six feet ten inches tall, with two little curls on either side of his bald pate – had grown gross and eccentric. As Princess Alice's daughter Victoria revealed many years later, Uncle Louis and her grandfather had endured strict discipline in their upbringing. When, for instance, they refused spinach and it was not all eaten for dinner, 'it was served for supper cold, and if some remained, it reappeared at breakfast the next day. To go to their rooms at night they had to walk unaccompanied down a long unlit passage and suffered agonies of terror from a tame raven which sometimes popped out on them.'

Whatever the cause, Grand Duke Louis's behaviour was rather bizarre in later life. With postillions and out-riders, he would often drive in his barouche and four to one of his country houses or shooting boxes. Ahead drove the cooks and food and his personal attendants, the brothers Fleck. One was his valet, one his hairdresser, and the third attended to his numerous pipes – a collection of ornately carved Meerschaum cigar-holders which, all numbered and catalogued, had to be smoked in rotation. Any new addition was smoked by Fleck the pipe-man until it matured. Most curious of all was his aversion to carrying a handkerchief. He rang a hand-bell when he wished to blow his nose, and the valet hurried in with a clean handkerchief on a salver, to which it was immediately returned after use. In all his homes save one, Louis kept an exclusive apartment with identical bedrooms: dark green wallpaper, mahogany furniture upholstered in green rep; novels and memoirs bound in black; a musical stand for cigars; and a packet of papyrus – stale tobacco wrapped in rice paper.

Somewhat stifled by the parochialism of her Hesse relatives, Alice welcomed the more liberal Battenbergs. At least, she would write after the initial meeting at Heiligenberg: 'The whole family are very amiable towards me and Prince Alexander is most amusing.' Vicky, the Crown Princess of Prussia, would also inform Queen Victoria: 'I have seen Prince Alexander of Hesse ... he is quite in love with Alice.' In time, however, Alexander would bitterly resent the English Princess's admiration of Bismarck's policy of Prussian domination in a Greater Germany. But it would not prevent the eventual marriage of her eldest daughter to his eldest son.

Meanwhile, the ties that bound the Battenbergs with the Romanoffs would predominate. It could not be otherwise considering the deep affection of the Tsarina Marie for her brother. Not even Alexander's banishment from Russia had impaired it. And after the Russian imperial family first invited themselves to stay at Heiligenberg in the summer of 1863, the annual 'invasion' became the cardinal event in the Battenberg calendar until the First World War.

In delicate health, the Tsarina looked upon Heiligenberg as a sanctuary from the acute strains of the St Petersburg Court. Originally it had been a peasant's farm, comprising a 'front house' and a 'back house' facing one another across a courtyard. Domestic and office buildings were eventually replaced by more magnificent structures. On the site of the 'back house' soared a great hall adjoining a massive terrace of lime trees, overlooking the spacious heights of the Klosterberg and the rich forests of Backhauser and Stettbach. In the far distance flowed the broad, impressive Rhine. Over the years Heiligenberg grew into an imposing *schloss*, with sixty rooms, surmounted by twin towers.

In adult life Prince Louis of Battenberg afforded a glimpse of those carefree days. 'Every summer,' he wrote, 'the Imperial family travelled into Germany. The Emperor first went to Ems to take the waters, whilst my aunt and her younger children came to the Heiligenberg. Here the Emperor ... later joined her, accompanied by one or another of his elder sons.' Then the Battenbergs, together with the tutor and governess, would evacuate their rooms and concentrate in the 'back house', while the imperial couple and their children 'moved into our proper rooms. The only member of the suite lodged at the Heiligenberg was the Mistress of the Robes, for many years Countess Pratassoff. The remainder of the large suite occupied villas and hotels in Jugenheim, but always drove up to the Heiligenberg for dinner at one and supper at eight o'clock.'

For dinner, served in the Garden Saloon, the gentlemen wore evening tail-coats with stars of orders, evening waistcoats, black bow ties and pearl-grey trousers. Frockcoats were worn for supper, served in the Terrace Saloon.

After the meal [Prince Louis continued] the long table was removed and card-tables set out, for '*Yeralash*', which is practically modern 'Bridge' but for the dummy hand. After the midday dinner, for which we children were admitted for dessert, the gentlemen played bowls, a very heating amusement which the Emperor delighted in. After a short siesta the carriages came round (our stables were filled up with horses from Uncle Louis's stables), and the family started off on an expedition to some place such as the '*Fürstenlager*' at Auerbach, Seeheim, the Frankenstein, Felsberg, etc, where '*Dick Milch*' (sour cream), tea or coffee was served.

The Emperor had a black retriever who used to take up a good deal of room on the floor of the open '*Korbwagen*' (literally a 'basket carriage'), in which the imperial couple and my parents always drove. Whenever the carriage passed a brook or pond, the dog used to jump out, plunge into it and return to the carriage. Neither my aunt nor my mother was allowed to say a word when the dripping, long-haired dog dried himself on their skirts, which in their amplitude was still reminiscent of the crinoline.

Sometimes the Heiligenberg reunion would be augmented with the children of the Crown Princess and, as the years passed, with the family of Princess Alice of Hesse. Like her sister Vicky, Alice horrified her august mother by breast-feeding her children herself – an act which evoked the indignant Queen's accusation of their making 'cows of themselves'. The parallel went further: a black Angus heifer at Balmoral was dignified by the name of 'Princess Alice'.

In time, and in varying degrees, some of these cousins would add their dramatic chapters to world history. By inter-marriage, fate would weave a vivid and rather complex pattern with their lives and even place them, through military conflict, in opposing dynastic clashes. Much of this intricate cousinhood originated from the affiliations of Princess Alice's children; indeed, the seeds of future romance were being sown in those Heiligenberg days. Prince Louis of Battenberg would seek the hand of Alice's daughter Victoria (Vicky), whose sister Elizabeth (Ella) would marry the Grand Duke Serge, the brother of Tsar Alexander III, who was the son of Prince Louis's aunt Marie of Hesse (the wife of Tsar Alexander II). Both Ella and Serge would be brutally murdered by revolutionaries, and a similar gory fate awaited Ella's sister Alexandra (Alicky) when she married Tsar Nicholas II, the son of Tsar Alexander III by his marriage to Dagmar, Princess of Denmark (the sister of Princess Alexandra who would wed the future Edward VII). The last ruler of Russia, Tsar Nicholas II, would be assassinated with his family at Ekaterinburg by Lenin's Bolsheviks in 1918. The fourth Hessian princess, Irene, would become the wife of Prince Henry of Prussia, brother of the egocentric Kaiser William of the First World War, and Ernest Louis, Alice's son, would create a further Hessian dynastic bridge by marrying another namesake of Queen Victoria – the daughter of Alfred, Duke of Edinburgh, and Marie, the daughter of Marie of Hesse and Alexander II.

This brief genealogical summary will suffice to illustrate the Battenbergs' special tie with Europe's royal houses of the last century. The intricacies of this relationship are incongruously highlighted when one realizes that Prince Louis of Battenberg's father-in-law was his first cousin; and that Marie, Duchess of Edinburgh, a Russian first cousin, was also his mother-in-law's sister-in-law and his brother-in-law's mother-in-law. As if to add to the confusion, when Louis's brother Henry (Liko) married Princess Beatrice, Queen Victoria's youngest daughter, the English Princess was not merely the aunt of Louis's wife but also her sister-in-law. Elizabeth of Hesse, another sister-in-law, was also the wife of his cousin, the Grand Duke Serge of Russia and, continuing the Russian connection, his sister-in-law Alicky became the consort of Tsar Nicholas II, his first cousin once removed.

The Battenbergs' gradual inter-marrying into the seats of power had a parallel in the Coburg dynasty some decades previously when, from relative obscurity, it rose to royal heights with the marriage of Queen Victoria – a Coburg herself on her mother's side – and her Coburg cousin Prince Albert. There was, however, one cardinal difference: the Battenbergs ultimately advanced because of distinguished soldiering, whereas the Coburgs had begun as minor sovereign dukes. In marriage they had been an ideal choice, because they were free from all commitments or bias in inter-dynastic rivalries.

Through their nine children, Victoria and Albert would convey their blood to more than half of the royal families of Europe. In some cases the results would be catastrophic. Tragically, their descendants would inherit haemophilia, a fearful disease of slow-clotting blood. A wound so easily led to death, and even a bruise could prove fatal by creating an internal haemorrhage. Gradually this frightful complaint would manifest itself as Queen Victoria's daughters and grand-daughters married into the Hessian, Hohenzollern, Romanoff, Teck, Battenberg and Bourbon families.

In the last century little was known about haemophiliacs save that the disease, transmitted by the female line, struck almost exclusively at the males – and occasionally generations later. It would be dubbed 'the royal disease', and Queen Victoria, profoundly shocked, would finally confess: 'Our poor family seems persecuted by this awful disease.' But was it not the dreadful truth that the Queen herself originated the malady? Or was it Albert? Prince Francis Joseph of Hohenlöhe, who studied records of families affected by haemophilia, concluded that the dread disease began with Queen Victoria herself. Since her Hanoverian father was not a victim, and since there was no trace in her Coburg mother's ancestry, Professor Haldane, stressing the absence of haemophilia in any of Victoria's uncles or male cousins, advanced the theory that a mutation occurred in the sperm cells of the Duke of Kent, her father.

Neither circumstantial evidence nor speculation has fully clarified the source of the hereditary taint. Indeed, for a period it seemed as if it had vanished as mysteriously as it came. Almost two decades had elapsed since the birth of the haemophiliac Leopold when his sister, Princess Alice, first noticed the tell-tale bruises and lumps on the body of her son 'Frittie', then eighteen months old. About a year and a half earlier, Alice had ecstatically informed her mother that her youngest and favourite child was fat, round and firm, 'with rosy cheeks and the brightest eye possible. He is very healthy and strong, and in fact the prettiest of all my babies'. Thus the tragic discovery was all the more disquieting and, moreover, like an echo of the past. Leopold – ironically

Princess Alice, one of Queen Victoria's daughters, who married Louis, the nephew of Prince Alexander of Hesse, and thus began the Hessian link by marriage with the British royal house.

The surviving children of Princess Alice with their father, Louis IV, and Queen Victoria, their grandmother. Victoria would be married to Prince Louis of Battenberg, Alicky to Tsar Nicholas II, Ella to the Grand Duke Serge, and Irene to Prince Henry of Prussia. Ernest's first wife would be Victoria Melita, daughter of the Duke and Duchess of Edinburgh.

one of Frittie's godfathers – had experienced similar symptoms at about the same age. When Alice wrote to Queen Victoria in despair, the matriarch expressed the plaintive hope that Frittie might 'out-grow this'. But death stalked him from birth; he would not even attain his third birthday.

Frittie was an energetic child, and it was with constant anxiety that Princess Alice tried to protect her lively son. But this was impossible. Cutting his ear early in 1872, the child bled profusely for three days until excruciatingly tight bandages and caustic finally stemmed the flow. Worse was to come in the next year.

On the delightfully sunny morning of 29 May, Frittie and his elder brother Ernest were chasing each other from window to window when Ernie disappeared in a sitting-room. The Princess went to ensure his safety, but on her return noticed, to her alarm, that Frittie had disappeared completely. Alice's fears were justified. Running to a window, she stared aghast on to the stone steps leading from the lower room into the garden. There, completely motionless, lay her ill-fated son. How the little boy had clambered through the window, no one would ever know, for the stone sill was tall enough to protect an adult. By the time the Princess had hurried below, an elderly housemaid had carried the unconscious Frittie indoors. A fractured skull and effusions of blood on the brain might have assured his death. Haemophilia made it inescapable.

The grief-stricken mother wrote to Queen Victoria: 'The horror of my Darling's sudden death at times torments me too much, particularly waking of a morning ... He was such a bright child. It seems so quiet next door. I miss the little feet, the coming to me, for we lived so much together.'

Alicky – one of Alice's daughters – after her marriage to Tsar Nicholas II, would distractedly watch her son in bouts of bleeding, quite powerless to help him. Irene, another daughter, the wife of Prince Henry of Prussia, Admiral of the Imperial German Fleet, would bear three sons – Waldemar, Heinrich and Sigismund. While they were playing trains in the castle at Kiel, Heinrich, in a moment of excitement, overbalanced a chair and crashed on to his head. It was not the blow that was fatal; he died sixteen days later of internal haemorrhage.

The fate of Waldemar would be harrowing and far more shocking. True, he lived to the age of fifty-six, residing at Schloss Kamenz in Upper Silesia, but he would be a frequent patient in the hospital at Kiel. Haemophilia had attacked him once again, enfeebling him severely, when, with his wife, Princess Calixta of Lippe, he fled before the all-conquering advance of the Russians in the Second World War. It was a circuitous and taxing route – even leading him as far as Prague – that eventually brought the Prince, who was critically weak, to Tutzing on the Starnberger Sea. The ordeal was quickly seen to be of no avail. The day after he received his first transfusion of blood, the American army over-ran that district, and all the medical resources were directed to ease the suffering of the inmates in a concentration camp. One cannot ignore the inhumanity of leaving Waldemar to die. The wretched Prince, whose genetic ailment had placed him aloof from hostilities, bled to death on 2 May 1945, and went to a pauper's grave in a rickety van – the only 'hearse' available.

Years earlier, when the broken-hearted matriarch learned of her son Leopold's death, she wrote sadly in her *Journal*: 'I am a poor, lonely old woman and my cup of sorrow runs over. Oh, may God in His mercy spare my other dear children ...' Only her own death would release her from the torment of further domestic trials, but even as her life ebbed on her death-bed, four grandchildren and great-grandchildren were already victims of the inherited disease. Her grand-daughter, the Tsarina Alicky, would labour under the chronic emotional strain caused by the Tsarevich, her haemophiliac son. When Victoria's daughter Beatrice married Henry of Battenberg, their daughter Victoria Eugénie would herself carry the disease and disastrously help to wreck Bourbon rule in Spain.

3

Privilege and its Drawbacks

ON 5 August 1868, while enjoying the bathing at Petersthal, Princess Marie of Battenberg received a letter from her father Prince Alexander. 'Mama', he wrote, 'will have told you I have acceded to Louis's wish, but with a heavy heart. I gave him twenty-four hours to think over it. The dear boy was very much affected, but stood by his decision, so I telegraphed to Osborne. God grant I may never regret letting him go to a foreign country.'

In conflict with the ancestral military tradition and (because he lived in landlocked Hesse) having scant knowledge of the sea, young Prince Louis – for no apparent reason – was obsessed with the desire to join Britain's Royal Navy. On occasions he had gazed on the sea off Italy, where he had learned to swim and manoeuvre a gondola, but that was all – scarcely the nautical background expected of the man who became one of the most brilliant naval tacticians of all time.

It is suspected that Queen Victoria's son Alfred, Duke of Edinburgh, a post-captain, fired Louis's passion for fighting ships. Then studying at the University of Bonn, sometimes visiting his sister Princess Alice in Darmstadt, he would regale Louis with stirring tales about naval life. Alice, in her turn, encouraged her husband's young cousin to choose a career at sea. But the notion appalled both Prince Alexander and Princess Julie. Louis's father suggested that he should seek a commission in the Austrian navy, but Louis argued that it was preferable to enter the mightiest navy in the world. Prince Alexander could not deny that Austria had been weakened by the Austro-Prussian war two years earlier. He had commanded the Eighth Army Corps of the German Federation, the sovereign German states that bore allegiance to the Emperor Francis Joseph. Indeed, the war, which ended in Austrian defeat, had even denuded Hesse of some territory; the northern region had been annexed by Bismarck's Prussia, including Battenberg, from which Alexander's family had derived its name. The Battenbergs themselves might have fared badly, too, but for the intervention of the Tsar, who threatened military reprisals if the Prussians molested Alexander's family and property.

In the First World War, when irresponsible tongues wrongly accused Prince Louis of pro-German sympathies, they failed to recall that as a boy of twelve he had witnessed his father go to war with the Prussians, who had mutilated and impoverished the lands of Hesse.

Once parental objections were overcome, Louis experienced the sort of privilege which, though easing at times the rigours at sea, would also militate against him. He had already passed his fourteenth birthday, the maximum age for entering the training ship *Britannia* as a cadet, but Princess Alice overcame this problem by writing to Queen Victoria, who tacitly arranged for the limit to be raised by six months. To prepare him for the examination at Portsmouth Naval College in December, a tutor from Magdalen College, Oxford, travelled to Darmstadt.

His Romanoff relatives were still installed at Heiligenberg when, on 25 September, after an emotional farewell, Louis set off for England accompanied by his father and tutor. Julie, in tears, believed she was bidding him goodbye for ever.

Up to December, Prince Louis lived with the family of Dr Burney, the owner of a private school at Gosport. But as well as lessons there were other matters to attend to, such as nationality and dress. To shed his German citizenship, he appeared before a public notary on 14 October, swearing allegiance to the matriarch on what he considered to be 'a very dirty Bible'. Until he possessed the appropriate dress, a visit to the Queen was out of the question. Recommended to Prince Alfred's tailor, Louis wrote to Princess Julie: 'Mr Burney and my tailor say that I cannot go to the Queen in my short Cadet jacket but must have what is called a Full Dress Coat ... with anchor buttons and a few other gold trifles.' As well as the uniform, there were the other odds and ends to collect: his dirk and sextant, his sea-chest and hammock and other items of a cadet's kit.

If Louis experienced qualms at the examination in December, they were quite groundless. The results were commendable. His long-sightedness gave him a little concern, but he countered it with quick-wittedness. Aware that he would be asked to read the time on the clock on the dockyard tower, he made certain of synchronizing his watch with the clock and snatched a look at it at the appropriate time.

Louis noted with pride that his name had been placed on the books of the *Victory*, Nelson's historic flagship, now flying the flag of the commander-in-chief at Portsmouth. He was now 'Cadet His Serene Highness the Prince Louis of Battenberg', but from the outset he was no ordinary cadet. Socially the royal aura was too dominant to allow it, yet it would have great disadvantages, too; privilege would even be obstructive in its way. Indeed, in the earlier years of his career, it was questionable if he was not more courtier than sailor, for royal influence imprinted itself from the beginning. The naval pundits had arranged that, in the New Year, Louis would by-pass the *Britannia* and receive his training at sea in the *Bristol*. But privilege intervened. In a training sense, the voyage round the world with 'Uncle Affie', which he had evaded, would have been preferable to what was in store. Princess Alice had written to her brother, the Prince of Wales, requesting him to treat the young Louis as his protégé. The future Edward VII responded with gusto, insisting that Louis should accompany him as an aide-de-camp on a Mediterranean cruise in the frigate *Ariadne*. The honour was extremely gratifying to a boy of fourteen, but he would soon learn that a penalty was involved.

Happily, Louis was able to spend Christmas with his family in Hesse; then in January he joined his ship at Trieste. Louis's introduction to the dark and stuffy gun-room – the midshipmen's quarters – merely 'had the one virtue of being warm'. Cramped and noisy, gun-rooms were by tradition abaft the men's quarters on the lower deck. Outside the midshipmen's mess lay their chests, over which they slung their hammocks at night. The food, which was similar to that in Nelson's day, was almost inedible. The salt beef was unusually tough, like the weevil-infested biscuits, and Louis found it hard to accustom himself to such a diet. How sharp the contrast when the Prince and Princess of Wales and their suite came aboard on the evening of 27 January 1869. Louis, the lamentably untrained recruit, sat with the royal party at dinner, when he was invited to take part in a cruise up the Nile. Thus deprived of normal training, fostering jealousy and alienation from fellow midshipmen, Louis later appreciated that his favoured treatment was 'a great mistake'.

Disembarking at Alexandria on 2 February, the royal party boarded the Nile flotilla at Cairo four days later. The cruise was on a lavish scale. Fitted with a special deck-house which served as a dining-saloon, and cabins for the greater part of the suite, a huge paddle-steamer towed a houseboat, also equipped with a roomy deck-house and cabins for their royal highnesses and their immediate entourage. A luxurious carpet covered the deck, and the furnishings – including the piano stool – were in blue silk. Astern of the houseboat came the kitchen-steamer where the meals were cooked – it also towed floating stables with Arab horses for the entire party, and a splendid white donkey for the Princess of Wales. Behind the kitchen-steamer came the provisions-carrier, heavy with exquisite foodstuffs and 1,000 bottles of champagne, 3,000 of claret, 10,000 of port and 20,000 of soda water.

Accompanied by auxiliary craft, this elaborate expedition began a tour of historic remains, and Louis, writing to his mother, explained: 'The enclosed piece of mummified material was given to me by the Prince of Wales.' Visits were interspersed with shooting, but Louis was forbidden to use a gun. He described the killing of flamingoes as mere slaughter. Crocodiles were immune until the Prince of Wales decided to use explosive bullets. Hyenas, recorded Louis, offered the most elusive targets. One moonlit night he and the Prince spent hours in hiding, using a freshly-killed kid as bait, but not a single hyena came near.

At his palace in Cairo, their host, the Khedive of Egypt, entertained the party in sumptuous style on their return. He was in fact treating the occasion as a rehearsal for the opening of the Suez Canal the following year.

From Cairo the party travelled by train to Suez to be welcomed by the canal's creator, Ferdinand de Lesseps, who lived in impressive manner near his gargantuan

Cadet Prince Louis of Battenberg (second from the left) with the Prince and Princess of Wales and their entourage after inspecting the new Suez Canal during a visit to Egypt.

Crown Princess Frederick of Germany and her son, the future Kaiser William II. The mother would favour the Battenbergs; at times the son would be openly hostile.

project. After entertaining the complete suite, he invited the Prince of Wales to open a ceremonial sluice to release the waters of the Mediterranean.

The party then sailed to Alexandria in the Khedive's palatial yacht, in which servants far outnumbered the guests. From Alexandria the *Ariadne* continued to the Dardanelles, where Louis assisted the Prince of Wales to fire marble shot – each weighing some six hundred pounds and ricocheting over the glass-like sea – from the huge muzzle-loaders that protected the straits. Then on to Constantinople for visits to the British Embassy and Saleh Bazar, the Sultan's palace. Next, over the Black Sea to Sebastopol, where Russian generals fêted the young cadet because of his father's connections with the tsarist army.

The party were conducted over the Crimean battlefields, and Louis, accompanying the Prince, galloped over the ground immortalized by the heroic charge of the Light Brigade at Balaklava. One night was spent at Livadia, the delightful villa owned by Louis's aunt, the Tsarina Marie.

Now homeward bound, the *Ariadne* dropped anchor at the Piraeus, where King George of the Hellenes was reunited with his sister the Princess of Wales. At dinner in Athens that evening – 'a very grand and picturesque affair, as all the servants were in Greek costume, called the *fustanella*' – the King induced Louis to smoke his first cigarette. Neither King nor cadet could possibly have imagined that their families would one day be united by marriage. Louis's daughter Alice, yet to be born, would enter the Greek royal house as the wife of George's son Andrew. The festivities included a week's stay on the beautiful island of Corfu, where Olga, the King's consort, had lately given birth to a son – Constantine – at the villa called 'Mon Repos'. Years hence, in the same royal residence, Alice would bear her only son, Prince Philip, Duke of Edinburgh.

Having basked in regal splendour for some weeks, when Louis was thrust unceremoniously into the gloom and severities of the gun-room, it came as a shock. His benefactors had left the *Ariadne* at Brindisi to return home by train. Lacking their protection, Louis, quite untrained, now felt the sobering blast of naval discipline. With no comforts to counter the harshness, bullying and even sadism of the gun-room, his ardour for the Royal Navy quickly waned. Maybe his German origin made him unpopular, and perhaps the recent favours had engendered envy, but he was overwhelmed. On arriving at Malta in utter despair, he wrote plaintively to his father to secure his release. He described 'the constant terror' when ordered aloft, terrified that he would be flung to his death at the next lurch of the ship.

When the *Ariadne* duly anchored at Spithead, it appeared that the Lords of the Admiralty – whether by negligence or design – had granted Louis his wish, for he was released from the navy. Having previously acceded to the Prince of Wales's instructions, the Admiralty now seemed indifferent to Louis's future. Lonely and confused, he wrote to the Prince of Wales who, inviting him to Marlborough House, advised him to 'stick it out'. One has no knowledge of any approach made privately by the Prince to their Lordships, but it is certain that Princess Alice communicated with Sir Sidney Dacres, the Senior Naval Lord.

Louis, then at Heiligenberg, was appointed to the *Royal Alfred*, flagship of the North American and West Indies Station – far from the misguiding influence of the Prince of Wales. Yet, on returning to London, he was allowed the use of a room at Marlborough House which would be available to him until his marriage in 1884.

The *Royal Alfred* was an old line-of-battleship converted into an ironclad before her construction had been finished. Most of the crowded gun-room lay below the water-line, so that little light penetrated three small scuttles set in the ship's side. The lamps had to be kept burning all day, and if these were out of order or broken, then the lighting was meagre, depending on small tallow candles called 'Purser's Drips' stuck into empty gin bottles.

In the main, the food in this twilight world was atrocious, the sub-lieutenants claiming by reason of rank the best of the unsavoury fare. But weevils and maggots in the biscuits, and cockroaches in the milk, were common to all. Most officers and cadets welcomed the traditional bottle of rum which was issued every ten days, but Louis, who drank no alcohol, traded his rum, officers permitting him to place the cost of extra food on their mess bills. But at one period even this was inadequate, leading to such a deterioration in his health that the ship's doctor informed the admiral. Louis was thus allowed to sleep in the admiral's quarters, was made an honorary member of the mess and within weeks was hale and hearty.

Although the usual period was three years, the commission of the *Royal Alfred* – due to a change of admirals – lasted four years and seven months. At least the long period ensured that Louis was trained in seamanship. From May to November the squadron was based at Halifax, Nova Scotia, sometimes emerging for target practice or a short cruise up the St Lawrence River to Quebec. As the spiteful cold approached, the admiral closed his official residence, embarking for the next six months to West Indian sunshine. With him went his household, including servants and grooms, horses and carriages and so much livestock – cows, sheep and poultry – that Louis described the main deck as being similar to a farm. This was fortunate for midshipmen of the middle watch, who surreptitiously milked a cow when brewing the cocoa.

In 1870, at the request of Prince Alexander of Hesse, the Admiralty granted Louis leave to return to Heiligenberg for his confirmation. A delighted Louis wrote to his father: 'Dearest beloved Papa, My mind is in a whirl and I can hardly think for joy. But I must pull myself together and try to express myself clearly. . . .'

Louis arrived home in mid-June – 'very brown and very tall, and with the least suggestion of a beard', wrote his sister Marie. The smell of Russian leather, the presence of the Cossacks and sentries and the Tsar's dog Punch, were signs that the Romanoff relatives were in residence. But they left for St Petersburg some days later, a few weeks before Prussia and France were locked in mortal conflict. Indeed, Louis's reunion with his family coincided with an atmosphere tense with the fear of war. The Battenbergs were extremely vulnerable, for through a telescope on one of the castle towers the distant frontier of France could be seen. Fearing that his horses might be seized by the army, Prince Alexander had them hidden in the neighbouring woods and prepared to have the family jewels and silver buried in the garden.

Already German mobilization had begun, and all the trains were commandeered. Soon there would be neither letter post nor telegrams until the authorities improvised a post on horseback.

Almost daily Louis and his brothers and sister drove to the station at Bickenbach to cheer the soldiers travelling to the frontier. Louis left his account of his impressions, but Princess Alice of Hesse, who for some years had been engrossed in nursing and hospital activity, wrote more graphically, explaining to Queen Victoria: 'I see daily, in all classes, so much grief and suffering; so many acquaintances and friends have fallen! It is heart-rending ... hourly the trains bring in fresh wounded, and many and shocking are the sights one sees ... I have still three hospitals for this afternoon.'

The winter cold came early that year, inflicting acute suffering on the peasants, who were impoverished by the war. Alice's daughter Vicky, who would one day be Louis's wife, helped her mother to distribute soup from the communal kitchens. She witnessed, too, the suffering of the wounded in the hospital huts in the palace grounds and the misery of the soldiers in their compounds.

Prince Alexander observed with mounting dismay Bismarck's relentless militarism crushing the French into defeat. It is on record that he secretly tried to induce the Emperor Francis Joseph and the King of Italy to rally to Napoleon III, but Austria had entered into a secret agreement with Prussia. More far-sighted than many – and certainly in contrast to what seemed to be British apathy – the Prince was conscious that out of Prussian conquest must arise a Prussian-dominated German empire which would be invincible in Europe. His fears were confirmed when the Emperor Napoleon surrendered at Sedan.

Not long before his confirmation, Louis, accompanied by his sister Marie, was allowed to visit Wilhelmshöhe, where the castle grounds were public, to see the captive Emperor. According to Marie, Napoleon 'liked to show himself, and when he rode through the gaping crowd he always, very affectedly, removed his hat, almost like the director of a circus in the arena.' Louis and Marie observed him through glasses. What they saw was a rather short man, round-shouldered and crooked – 'but he walked as gracefully as a dancing-master, holding his head on one side. His hair was grey and much pomaded, his moustache and beard fair, his eyes blue and very piercing ... At the royal stables his groom showed us the horses he rode at Sedan.'

This was the monarch who, at the zenith of his power, had conducted diplomatic discussions with Louis's father. As he observed the defeated Emperor, Louis did not know that he was witnessing the beginning of a significant new chapter in European history that would embroil him in personal disaster little more than four decades later.

Indeed, Napoleon's capitulation would be seen as a major turning point in world history. The eclipse of one sovereign contrasted vividly with the meteoric rise to power of the King of Prussia who was now proclaimed the Kaiser of a German Reich. The First World War would draw nearer as an arrogant Germany, already sated with power, sought greater aggrandizement.

Each year Prince Louis's squadron adhered to a pattern that rarely changed, but in the West Indies visits ashore – notably to the grand balls at each of the islands – helped to relieve the monotony of peacetime naval life. In Louis's case, his royal connections made him popular wherever he went, not only with white hostesses but with coloured people as well.

It appears that the companionship of his shipmates was not congenial. Louis was artistic, but his fellow midshipmen were decidedly not. Louis was keen on intellectual discussion, but the others – described as being of a hunting-and-shooting background – had no idea what intellectualism was.

Louis corresponded regularly with his family, but his letters indicate that it was to his sister Marie – who had now married Gustavus I of Erbach-Schönberg – that he unburdened himself in his darker moods. Perhaps the reason for his impetuous out-pourings was home-sickness. His desire to see Hesse had possibly been stimulated by the arrival of HMS *Challenger*, then sailing on a world voyage of scientific discovery, for among her personnel was the distinguished German professor Baron von Willemoes-Sohn, with whom Louis liked to converse.

I felt very clearly [Louis wrote to Marie after the *Challenger* had left] why it is that I am beginning to find it so dull in the English Navy; it is because of the lack of anyone with whom I could have a good talk – in a word a friend. That's why I long to be with my own countrymen. I have not yet found a friend among the many comrades I have had in the 'R.A.' [*Royal Alfred*]; and senior officers will always be senior officers, particularly on board ship. So I am thrown entirely on my own resources, and although I have, in time, become accustomed to many things, I shall never feel quite at home in the English Navy.

This attitude was obviously merely a passing phase, for in the same letter he admits that some of his happiest hours were spent aboard the *Royal Alfred*. Years afterwards, Prince Louis came to appreciate that the sturdy foundations of his career were laid not in the *Ariadne* but aboard the *Royal Alfred*. Moreover, some of his fellow midshipmen – in some instances rising high in the naval hierarchy like himself – would remain intimates for the rest of his life. Prominent were Francis Spring-Rice, Charles Cunningham Graham and Salis Schwabe. Among that turbulent fraternity, Schwabe seems to have been the closest friend, accompanying Louis to New York – a trip achieved through the generosity of Aunt Marie in Russia. In the autumn of 1871, when the *Royal Alfred* docked in Quebec, the two young midshipmen continued up the St Lawrence River to Montreal in a three-storey paddle-steamer. Next they travelled by train to

Toronto and then to Niagara, returning to Montreal by steamer, exhilarated by that stage of the journey when the flat-bottomed vessel occasionally bumped the river bed in negotiating the Lachine Rapids.

The contradictory character of Louis's letters suggests some instability at this period. To imply that he was thrown on his own resources was mere hyperbole, for no one in the squadron was in such social demand. Typical was the arrival of his Romanoff cousin Alexei, then serving in the frigate *Svetlana* and on an official visit to Havana. Various festivities were arranged in honour of the Grand Duke Alexei Alexandrovich, and Prince Louis was always a guest.

Before he left Canadian and Caribbean waters, Louis had become signal mate, as senior midshipman. This was the stage when he first exhibited the technical ingenuity which marked his later career (a skill which would eventually be manifest in his younger son, Louis). Prince Louis was admired for the way in which he handled a primitive and intricate morse-signalling lamp which had been accepted by the Royal Navy. He developed it as a vital means of communication between ships at sea.

On his return to Europe in January 1874, privilege again threatened to disrupt his naval career. The Prince and Princess of Wales greeted him enthusiastically at Sandringham, a welcome which was equalled in London by that of his cousin Marie and Uncle Affie, who had recently married in St Petersburg – a union which reflected the persuasive powers of Prince Alexander of Hesse, for Queen Victoria had firmly opposed the marriage. Certain aspects of Affie's life had given his mother concern. He drank heavily – in fairness, a common trait of his times – and his liaisons were not infrequent. Indeed, at the time he was in Darmstadt expatiating to Louis on the attractions of naval life, his affairs stirred the watchful matriarch to question Hessian 'love of society'.

Anxiety, however, had been replaced by annoyance when the Queen was told of Affie's enthusiasm for the Tsar's daughter. Victoria shuddered at the thought of a union with the detestable Romanoffs. The possibility, however, had been discussed when the German, Russian and British relatives assembled at the wedding of Princess Marie of Battenberg. Reluctance to give their consent was just as ingrained in Prince Alexander's sister and brother-in-law, but love and diplomacy triumphed. For the Grand Duchess Marie's dowry, the Russian Government supplied a million roubles, which were augmented by the Tsar by another 600,000 roubles, yielding an annual income of £32,000 for Affie and his wife, an incredible sum in Victorian days.

Now that the Battenbergs were securely entrenched in the Russian and British Courts, Louis could not escape from the festivities that followed the arrival of the newly-weds in Britain, such as the weekend spent at Osborne when members of Queen Victoria's family gathered to meet the Edinburghs. Buckingham Palace was the setting of much gaiety. Afterwards, Queen Victoria, writing to Prince Alexander of Hesse, thanked him for effecting a *rapprochement* between the Courts at St Petersburg

Queen Victoria championed the Battenbergs, allowing one to marry a daughter and another a grand-daughter. She is shown here in Darmstadt with other royalties.

Prince Louis of Battenberg, who became a naturalized Briton when he joined the Royal Navy. His daughter, Alice, would be the mother of Prince Philip, Duke of Edinburgh.

and London, adding that she would maintain her interest in his son Louis, 'who ... is doing extremely well in the Navy'.

Her interest amounted to observing the young officer closely, noticing how his charm attracted her daughter Beatrice. While dining at Osborne, the Princess, placed next to him, had greatly puzzled Louis by remaining singularly inarticulate. Not until years later did he appreciate the cause; not wishing to lose her daughter through marriage, the Queen had instructed Beatrice to be silent, a warning to Louis that she was not a potential bride. The attentive Beatrice had grown indispensable to the Queen, who was determined to retain her services. To enforce her will, Victoria made the Admiralty aware that Louis's posting to some foreign station would not be unacceptable.

This, as time would indicate, would have been no disservice to Prince Louis. Already the glittering social scene was dangling its temptations before him, distractions that were preferable to the rigours of the gun-room. He was now engaged on a course at the Royal Naval College at Greenwich and the exacting social round proved irresistible. In consequence, the result of his examination for sub-lieutenant fell below his normal standard. The president, the formidable Admiral Sir Astley Cooper Key, had earlier warned him of his folly. The fact that he had secured only a second galvanized Louis to more strenuous efforts; in further courses, he passed out first (and the best student ever) at seamanship, and first (and joint best student) at gunnery. He should have achieved a first for French but received only a second. Louis, who was extremely fluent in the language, was amazed until he discovered that the French examiner had learned that his German family had participated in the Franco-Prussian war.

Released from his intensive studies, Louis now enjoyed with unbridled enthusiasm the balls and receptions, hunting and shooting. The royal occupants of Marlborough House were the source of many of these delights. The Prince of Wales had Louis appointed a member of the Marlborough Club – for which Prince Alexander received an account for the £42 subscription – and later confided in his young friend that he was to visit India that winter. He invited Louis to accompany him.

After the débâcle of the Indian Mutiny, British power was approaching its zenith in the vast sub-continent. The visit of Queen Victoria's heir in 1875–6 was a physical sign of that material might, for the tour was conducted on a scale that erred on the side of the grandiose. Extreme pomp is unfashionable nowadays, but to the Victorians it was the adrenalin that stirred the nation's pulse. They loved to see their future king strutting in spectacular ceremonial, and criticized the Queen for remaining in seclusion.

Prince Louis kept a detailed account of that tour which was essentially peculiar to the age. He himself was witnessing the strengthening of imperial authority with which he was happy to identify himself, yet ironically his future son – Earl Mountbatten of Burma – would be the person who, deputed by the Attlee Labour Government, would unravel that intricate skein some seven decades later.

The imperial sun still blazed high, however, as the *Serapis*, a converted India

34

troopship which the Prince and his retinue had joined at Brindisi, reached Calcutta on Christmas Eve. It was the beginning of an exotic journey that would take the royal party on a tortuous route of some seven thousand miles. For part of the distance – when the entourage would not resort to elephants or horses – the government had prepared a special train. Two of the carriages were devoted exclusively to the Prince of Wales: one for sleeping in and the other for daytime use. Adjoining was a dining-room car and beyond that were the sleeping cars, in which travelled the valets and luggage. The seniors (who included Prince Louis) were arranged in pairs, the remainder in fours. 'I shared a carriage', wrote Louis, 'with old Lord Alfred Paget, who snored terribly.' In the morning Louis watched his lordship dyeing his moustache with an old toothbrush. A bottle of brandy always stood beside his bed, and he habitually woke up during the night to smoke a cigarette.

Wherever the royal party went, there was an element of the exotic. For their spectacular visits the native princes drove in state carriages of fantastic design, escorted by uniformed bodyguards wearing ancient armour. The magnificence was enhanced by exquisitely ornamented elephants.

On the day of the reception [wrote Prince Louis] the princes, with their attendants on horse or foot, would be drawn up on a dusty highroad from early morning in strict order of precedence, and patiently wait by the hour for their turn. The return visits were most picturesque. As their palaces were generally too far away, the visit was returned in their encampments in the most gorgeous tents conceivable, hung with embroideries, the tent poles and furniture sometimes covered with silver, with wonderful carpets spread on the ground.

The Prince of Wales and the Maharajah would occupy temporary thrones at one end of an enormous Shamiana tent, with their respective suites sitting in rows at right angles to their masters. 'Attah and Pan' were then handed round; the former (scent) was so pervading that a special handkerchief was kept to receive it – 'and with which one might afterwards have run a drag'. The visitors were then decorated with flower wreaths hung like collars round their necks. On this occasion real presents were exchanged, not merely presented and given back. Thus the Prince of Wales had brought with him silver statuettes, gold cups, guns and jewelled swords. 'In intrinsic value,' explained Louis, 'there was of course no comparison, as HRH often received jewels and pearls for his wife of fabulous value and on which some Maharajahs spent a whole year's income. Live animals were often included . . . a full-grown tiger was led in by four powerful men, two holding a collar round the animal's neck, the others round the loins. The beast nearly trod on my toes and gave me rather a start.'

The grandeur of the three-day stay at Benares was incredible. There being no house big enough to accommodate the entire party, the upshot was a mushroom settlement of luxurious tents which housed facilities for every possible need. Consummate care was taken to cater for personal desire and comfort. Louis described how, after wining and dining in full measure one evening, each member of the royal suite returned to his 'enormous divan with many soft cushions. Refreshments and smoking material were laid out on a little table. On the divan reclined a native girl in transparent white garments'.

Louis was exhilarated by the dangers and skills involved in pig-sticking. The spear was so sharp that it could pierce through its victim with the slightest effort. Indeed, Louis was informed of a recent accident concerning two officers of the 10th Hussars: colliding violently at full gallop, one had skewered the other without realizing it. Louis himself had a very nasty accident.

At last I got so near to the prey [he wrote] that I dropped my spear down for the attack; that is, held it about the centre nearly horizontal at the full extent of the arm held vertically downwards. From that moment I remember nothing more. My horse went back to the bungalow very badly cut and bleeding ... Towards sunset I was found at the bottom of a deep *nullah*, with nearly vertical stone sides, insensible, with my crushed helmet near by: it had saved my head ... A mounted messenger was sent to Agra, and about midnight the Prince's doctor arrived and did me up. It was a broken collar-bone, but my brain was somewhat shaken, and my head ached badly.

While Louis was convalescing the Prince of Wales's party left for a great shooting expedition in the Terai. Fretting to take part in the hunt for tigers, Louis and his companions set off to join the others. The final stage of the journey was through jungle in *doolies* – coffin-like structures on two bamboo poles each carried by four men. On one side a sliding door enabled one 'to crawl in and lie down full length on a thin mattress, which was not very comfortable with my left arm across my body under my coat. The night was bitterly cold. Sleep was impossible as the *doolie* bearers kept up a jog-trot, chanting a dismal tune. The torches carried on each side blew their smoke into my box and nearly choked me'. A man-eating tiger had been reported in the district, so the natives had more torches and sang more raucously than usual. 'Of course,' explained Louis, 'there was quite a procession of these *doolies*, for which double teams were provided, which relieved each other in the shafts every half-hour, both teams running side by side.' At six in the morning, Louis reached the shooting camp, which crossed into Nepal the same day. There, in mammoth hunts, some eight hundred elephants were employed as beaters; among them were the privileged few (including Louis), namely, the guns.

Describing his first shot at a tiger, Louis explained: '... we were advancing on each side of a shallow *nullah*, thickly grown with bush. A tiger was known to be in this, so that I was told that if he broke cover on my side to fire. Before long he did so, at a great pace. I fired and missed. At the same moment my elephant saw the beast and in his fright whisked round on his hind legs. The Prince, very quick, put a bullet into him. I felt awfully disgusted.'

Louis had used a double-barrelled rifle for the first time, and his left arm was not yet equal to the strain. Yet three days later he made his first kill. The tiger

had been marked down in the high grass, clear of the woods, and it was very exciting following with a very frightened and unwilling elephant the movements in the high grass ahead of me ... Presently the movement ceased, but my animal refused to go near the spot. That fine old sportsman, Jung Bahadur [the Prime Minister] came and took me across into his *howdah*. The tiger allowed us very nearly to tread on him, though we could see nothing, when he suddenly, with a fierce roar, jumped straight at the elephant's right shoulder. We literally looked into each other's eyes as I gave him a bullet between his. Of course, the elephant flew off to the left, and the tiger lay once more hidden in the high grass. We approached again, but this time ... I gave him a second bullet in his head. We afterwards found that my first bullet had glanced along the skull under the skin, as I shot downwards as he was looking up.

Louis did not allow his love for the hunt to eclipse his interest in the wider world in which he travelled. Writing to his parents from Nepal, he referred to it as an independent kingdom ruled by a puppet king, the real head being Bahadur – 'who has had a curious career. In 1846 he was a simple infantry captain in the Nepalese Army; then he conceived the grand idea of taking over the government. To do this he invited about 30 of the highest of the land to a party at his house, had the house surrounded by his soldiers and shot down the entire company with his own hands with his hunting-rifle. The King was thus frightened into making him Prime Minister ...'

The Indian tour also enabled Louis to commercialize his talent for drawing. The *Illustrated London News* artist was instructed by his editor in Britain to proceed to China when the entourage embarked homeward at Bombay. Louis readily consented to deputize, sketching the final scenes before the *Serapis* left India, and produced an amazing pictorial record of a remarkable collection of animals which had been presented to the Prince.

Before the Prince of Wales left for the hunting in the Terai, he handed Louis two letters – one written by Uncle Affie in St Petersburg and the other by Prince Alexander, who was then visiting his sister Marie. Both requested him to accompany the Duke of Edinburgh in the *Sultan* which Affie was to commission for the Mediterranean in a few months' time. The hedonistic Prince of Wales tried to dissuade Louis from accepting, appealing to him 'to get a little half-pay and spend the season with me at Marlborough House'. But Louis wisely ignored these pleas.

Not that social life was lacking in Malta. Officers were joined by their families, and naval routine was planned to adhere where possible to the social pattern. Louis developed an enthusiasm for polo which he later passed on to his son Louis. Where facilities allowed, there was horse-racing and hunting, fishing and shooting. Banquets were held on board and ashore, and a unique innovation was the despatch, at great cost, of a pack of beagles from England. The battleship *Agincourt* accommodated the livestock, and the quick dismantling of kennels and stables, along with the ponies and dogs, became a serious facet of emergency tactics.

This exercise was charged with reality when war broke out in the Balkans in 1877. In her expansionist policy, Russia had attacked Turkey, whom Britain supported as a bulwark against Russian imperialism. As the Russian forces – despite earlier reverses – fought their way to Constantinople, the British fleet was ordered to prevent entry into the Turkish capital. Sandro, Louis's younger brother, now with the army commanded by the Tsar's brother, the Grand Duke Nicholas, informed his parents: 'This morning I rode with the Grand Duke ... up to the heights of San Stefano, and we saw Constantinople before us ... Tears filled the Grand Duke's eyes.' But the Russians knew that to go further would unleash the fury of the British naval guns.

The Turks surrendered, but the treaty signed at San Stefano was a precarious peace, and the Battenberg brothers' ingenuous behaviour at this unsettled period created much embarrassment. With Uncle Affie's approval, Louis arranged a reunion with Sandro in Constantinople, then invited him on board, taking him even to the *Temeraire* with its secret equipment. The Admiral of the British fleet was clearly embarrassed. For obvious reasons the Duke of Edinburgh and Louis had sympathy with Russia, and, after entertaining them to dinner in the flagship, the Admiral was relieved to see the Battenbergs leave for the Russian headquarters.

The pro-Turkish British ambassador in Constantinople, fearing that the peace negotiations might be endangered, wrote angrily to London. In a letter, Queen Victoria furiously upbraided her son.

[It] was most *injudicious* & *imprudent* [she wrote to Prince Alfred], and you will hear of it from the Admiralty. Alexander Battenberg may be very discreet & no doubt is very honour-able, but *how* can *you* think that the *officers* & *men* of our Navy and in the Fleet of which you are a Captain will *ever believe* that the *important secrets* will not be divulged? Anyhow, will they ever trust you & Louis Battenberg? I own I should hardly believe you *capable* of such imprudence & want of (to say the least) *discretion*. I will give you credit for its being an act of *extreme thoughtlessness*, but that for a Captain in command of a ship, that Captain the Sovereign's Son & at *such* a moment, when we don't know if we may not very soon be at war, is a very serious thing. And I fear the profession will not put so favourable a construction on your act, Louis Battenberg's prospects will be seriously injured by it & I don't see how he can or ought to continue to serve in the same ship with you ...

Louis, whose action had been motivated by fraternal affection, was transferred to another ship, and the *Sultan* was ordered home. The Tsarina Marie, writing to her brother, Prince Alexander of Hesse, referred to the Queen as 'a crazy old hag'. Angered by the royal strictures, Louis felt inclined to resign from the navy at once, and his father, incensed by the matriarch's comments, was tempted to agree. But gradually the Queen was pacified, and the breaches were healed.

On his return to London, Victoria invited Prince Louis to lunch, and he was received 'most graciously'. Tartly, Louis's aunt Marie contended that it was only necessary to give 'the old fool' a 'good fright to make her draw in her horns'. Louis, this time accompanied by his brother Sandro, was invited to Balmoral the following year. It opened a new chapter in the Battenberg story.

4

Balkan Political Quicksands

FOUR crowns had evaded Prince Alexander of Hesse. For his son Sandro it would be different, though the outcome would be an amalgam of drama and humiliation. After the Russo-Turkish war, the complex Treaty of Berlin of 1878, which had liberated Bulgarians from the Ottoman yoke, had enforced a division of that country; one detects Bismarck's machinations here. While northern Bulgaria was ostensibly to become an autonomous principality, with the Sultan of Turkey still claiming suzerainty, in practice – thus instilling fear in Britain and Austria – Alexander II welcomed it as a Russian satellite. It was part of the Iron Chancellor's scheme for Prussian expansion, preserving amity with the Tsar while creating foundations for a Greater Germany.

Sandro was drawn into the game of Balkan politics, with himself played as the pawn. His candidature as the new Sovereign Prince of Bulgaria was accepted by the respective powers as the most suitable of all for a number of reasons: he had connections with the English Court, was a German prince, the son of an Austrian general, a favourite nephew of the Tsar, was closely allied to Russia in virtue of his participation in the campaign of 1877–8, and yet was not a Russian. His choice would therefore please not only Disraeli and Bismarck, but Austria and Russia as well.

To Sandro, then twenty-two, the political quicksands in which he might founder were horrifying. He was in Berlin, having rejoined the Prussian *Gardes du Corps*, when the proposal was first made to him. Queen Victoria later recorded the meeting between the inflexible Bismarck and the hesitant Prince. 'Sandro', she wrote, 'went to him saying, he did not wish to accept the offer, & thought someone older would be better, upon which Pce Bismarck shut the door, & told him, he would not let him out, before he promised to accept. Sandro asked, what would happen, should he fail, as his whole future would be ruined, & he answered, "You will at all events take away a pleasant recollection with you." This made us all laugh.'

Both Prince Alexander of Hesse and Princess Julie shared their son's misgivings. They knew that Bismarck's motive in supporting Sandro's nomination was not to further Battenberg fortunes. Prince Alexander censured Bismarck's ambitions for Prussian domination in central Europe, and as his daughter Marie ultimately revealed

Kaiser William II, with whom Prince Louis was on familiar terms. The British Government availed itself of Louis's knowledge of matters concerning Germany and Russia.

Tsar Alexander II (seated) and (left to right) the Grand Duke Courland, the Grand Duchess Marie, and Alfred, Duke of Edinburgh, who was an intimate of the Battenbergs.

in her *Reminiscences*, Bismarck could not cast off the obsession of a 'Polish spectre' which he feared above all things from the Battenberg family. She wrote:

He saw with obstinate persistence, in Sandro particularly, but also in the other members of the Battenberg family, the possible occupant of the restored Polish throne. He carried this idea so far as to assert that Princess Beatrice of England, my brother Henry's wife, had in her suite a Polish monk in order to acquire the Polish language, which in our family is obligatory. We were often amused by this attitude, until we learned by bitter experience what it meant for Sandro to be exposed to Bismarck's personal vindictiveness ... Bismarck honoured my mother, who never had anything at all to do with politics, with a quite particularly suspicious interest, and always kept her under observation, merely because she was Polish by birth, and he ignored with iron persistence the fact that she was, thanks to her upbringing in Petersburg, a most loyal adherent of Russia. She belonged, involuntarily, to the women of princely rank whom the great Imperial Chancellor viewed with apprehension. When King Albert of Saxony came in 1890 for the first time to Darmstadt, he asked to be driven to Heiligenberg that he might make the acquaintance of the woman, then living there as a widow in profound solitude, 'of whom Bismarck was afraid'.

Personal disaster was virtually assured from the start, for Sandro had confided in his sister that he had no desire to ascend the Bulgarian throne 'out of consideration for the wishes of our Russian relatives', adding: 'Every happiness in life would then be over for me, for if I were to go, I should serve Bulgarian interests alone, and not those of Russia, and that Russia would never forgive.' Such sentiments were subsequently reaffirmed to Queen Victoria who loathed the Romanoffs ('... Russia is *our real enemy* & totally antagonistic to *England*').

On 29 April 1879 Sandro was elected by the National Assembly as Bulgaria's Sovereign Prince. In May, before the Bulgarian deputies assembled at Livadia in the Crimea, the Tsar himself placed the crown on his godson's head. Alexander's tears and embraces sealed Sandro's destiny.

Under the treaty, Sandro was compelled to visit the signatory nations in turn. Thus, travelling by night train with his brother Louis, he was welcomed by Queen Victoria at Balmoral on 6 June. That was their first meeting since he was five years old, and the Queen-Empress noted: 'Sandro ... is not very like his brother, much taller, 6 foot 2, dark, more like his mother, broad, & with a very good figure, a very open, good-natured face, good looking, but hardly as much as his brother Louis, who is 3 years older ... Both Sandro & Louis are so amiable, intelligent, & nice, so well brought up.' Between them the brothers dispelled all fears that Sandro might become pro-Russian, an assurance that later provoked the Tsarina Marie to observe 'that Brown [Queen Victoria's Scottish gillie who was suspected abroad as being her lover] has deigned to approve of the new Bulgaria and of Sandro'.

Wearing the *kolpak*, the traditional Bulgarian peasant cap, Alexander of Battenberg rode on horseback into Sofia, committed to 'the mission of piloting Bulgaria towards a happier future'. The squalor in his capital symbolized how formidable this task would be – a capital of unpaved streets and open sewers, and hovels everywhere. The ruined cathedral, converted into a mosque under Turkish rule, rose out of this dreary scene. The *konak*, Sandro's residence – lately occupied by Prince Dondukov-Korsakov, the Russian governor – was a decaying two-storey house in which a wooden staircase led to the private suite: a work-room, a drawing-room and Sandro's bedroom, where the roof leaked so badly that a canopy sprawled over the bed to ward off the rain. Angered because he himself had not been chosen to rule, Dondukov had petulantly taken the furniture – even the enamelled bath, which was now replaced by one of tin. Furniture from Heiligenberg and a Vienna store helped to rid the suite of its bareness.

What served as state rooms were also badly furnished. In the throne-room, where Sandro would receive dignitaries, a smattering of card-tables were left over from the late occupant's gambling parties.

Most of the people were illiterate, corruption was commonplace, and profound disagreements divided the more educated minority; one element allied themselves with tsarist aims for a 'little Russia', while others campaigned for Bulgarian freedom. Such were the prevailing conditions from which Sandro was expected to create a viable nation. The odds were against him from the outset; the constitution was too liberal for a nation which was tribal, and Russian infiltration had control of power. 'All the scum of Russia', Sandro informed his father, 'has taken refuge here and has tainted the whole country.' Moreover, Russian officials and army officers were intriguing to undermine his aim for more national liberty.

Prince Alexander suggested that Sandro should enumerate his problems to the Tsar in person, preparing a sixteen-page memorandum for his son, and with the dual purpose of also visiting his invalid sister journeyed to St Petersburg with his son Louis in February 1880. Their train was delayed – a factor which foiled an attempt to destroy the Tsar.

Although Alexander 11 was genuinely anxious to ease the life of the peasants, there were forces who were fanatical in their obsession to obliterate him. Although autocratic, he displayed more tolerance than either his predecessor or his successor, yet in spite of this, the determination of the Nihilists to assassinate him was never relaxed. In their fanaticism they had grown reckless; quite brazenly, the chief of police had been fatally stabbed in broad daylight, and the assassin escaped. His successor had been fortunate, evading death. So, too, had the Tsar himself, four shots failing to kill him even at close range; in the confusion, as guards slashed at the Nihilists with their swords, a fifth bullet had merely wounded Alexander in the foot. Further efforts to destroy the Tsar while travelling in his train had been equally abortive.

Now, on that reunion in February 1880, the Nihilists planned mass destruction. Posing as a workman in the basement of the Winter Palace, a carpenter named Stephen Chalturin secreted explosives under the guard-room which lay below the dining-hall. The conspirators, however, never considered that the train carrying Prince Alexander and his son might be late. The Tsar, accompanied by the Grand Dukes, was due to dine with his guests at 7.30, and the fuse was timed to reap large-scale death at eight o'clock. But everyone was still proceeding to the banquet when the terrifying explosion shattered the guard-room.

Writing to Princess Julie, Alexander explained: 'Everything was enveloped in a thick cloud of smoke and dust, the floor shook under our feet, the gas jets flared high for the moment, and then all was covered in darkness.' And in the darkness came the screams and groans of the wounded and dying; others had been crushed to death. But for the fortuitous escape of Prince Alexander and his sons, Battenberg – and European – history would have changed that night.

Sandro's talks in St Petersburg did not lessen his frustrations in Sofia, and events worsened a situation which finally grew untenable. Frail throughout her life, and now withered by tuberculosis, his aunt, the Tsarina Marie, died in June 1880 in abject loneliness. Her death ended prolonged unhappiness and humiliation, arising from her husband's liaison with his onetime ward, Catherine Dolgoruki; having borne him three children, the Tsar's concubine had long been installed on another floor in the Winter Palace. Alexander II had befriended Catherine since childhood – from the time that her father, Prince Michael, had frittered away his family's fortune. Despite the difference in their ages, a love affair had blossomed at Court, rousing not only Marie's but Prince Alexander's displeasure. 'Do you understand, my dear brother, that I love them both, our Marie and my little Katie?' the Tsar had pleaded with his brother-in-law.

Over the years, Prince Alexander had reconciled himself to the situation but he must have resented the Tsar's flaunting of his mistress. There had been, for instance, the incident in 1867 when, invited by Napoleon III to the World Exhibition, the Tsar had travelled with Alexander to Paris. Even Napoleon had been shocked when the Tsar welcomed Catherine to the Elysée Palace. Prince Alexander, who was waiting for his wife, promptly advised her to remain in Hesse. 'It would not be decent for a respectable woman to share the company of the Tsar's courtesan,' he wrote.

Prince Alexander learned of his sister's death from the Tsar, who, whatever his emotions, married his mistress within weeks, creating her Princess Yourievski, then sought to make her Empress. But an assassin's bomb destroyed himself and his plans.

In St Petersburg the revolutionaries strove relentlessly to kill the Tsar. First, the Nihilists rented a grocer's shop from which to tunnel under Sadovaya Street – the Tsar's normal processional route – but bombs, concealed in butter kegs, twice failed to kill him. Then, returning from the St Michael's barracks on 13 March 1881, good fortune deserted him. Stepping from the wreckage created by a parcel-bomb hurled on the Katherine Embankment, he would have survived but for a Nihilist, named Grinevitsky, who threw another bomb from close range. It smashed both legs and crushed the Tsar's left side, yet still he managed to murmur: 'Quick, home... take me home to die... not here.'

In her memoirs, Princess Marie of Battenberg relates how her father first learned of his brother-in-law's murder. Her parents were attending a performance of a Wagner opera at the Darmstadt Theatre, and she and her husband decided to join them. 'On the table in the entrance hall of the palace lay a telegram addressed to my father,' she recalled. 'I took it with me to the theatre. The second act was already in progress as we entered the box... I listened for a while to the music... and then gave my father the telegram... He read it and, deathly pale, staggered out into the salon. Horrified, we followed him. It informed him of the frightful murder of the Tsar – and my hand had brought the news to the theatre!'

Five years earlier, at Schönberg, her home, the Tsar had presented Marie with a brooch containing two diamonds and a pointed black pearl. 'See, this is quite a peculiar pearl I am giving you,' he explained, 'it is shaped like a bullet, a grenade. Think of me always when you wear it; it has much meaning.' Not until long after this last farewell did Marie learn of the Tsar's liaison with Catherine Dolgoruki. She wrote that one day, while at Heiligenberg,

one of the gentlemen of the Darmstadt Court said to me as I wished him good morning, 'Oh! I have seen you already this morning, when you were walking down in the valley with the Tsar, and your little son.' I denied having met him, but I was rather surprised, as I had been at home all the morning, and my little four-year-old son was at Schönberg. Only after the Tsar's departure did my mother tell me who the young lady, who was so like me, and the little boy were. Then something died in me.

The deaths of the Tsarina Marie and Alexander II loosened the close ties between the Battenbergs and the Romanoffs. Alexander III, the antithesis of his father, had a pronounced penchant for Pan-Slav ideas and was distinctly anti-German. A glimpse of his mean-spirited character had been revealed in a scene at Schönberg. Himself a connoisseur, he had displayed keen interest in the china collection owned by Princess Marie and her husband. To convince himself that it was not bogus, he deliberately broke a plate at table across his knee, then remarked: 'Why the china is really genuine!'

Alexander III does not appear to have harboured nostalgic memories of childhood visits to his Battenberg cousins. His hostility towards the choice of Sandro for the Balkan throne was well known; he had favoured Prince Valdemar, his Danish brother-in-law. The treacheries of Balkan politics and the Tsar's personal animosity would even wreck Sandro's romance with the princess he wished to marry. While in the Prussian *Gardes du Corps*, Sandro had formed an attachment for Princess Vicky of Prussia, the daughter of Crown Prince Frederick and Crown Princess Victoria. The affection was mutual, but the friction it engendered would earn its place in history as the 'Battenberg Affair'. Initially, only the Crown Princess knew of the match, and she encouraged it, but gradually Bismarck's secret police probed the letters that passed between Potsdam and Sofia. Such a union did not fit in with Bismarck's plans. However, his ill-will towards the Battenbergs, who, like the Coburgs years before them, were acquiring power through marriage, would be minimal when set against the Tsar's antagonism if the betrothal persisted.

Sandro learned how formidable were the obstacles towards marriage when he sought the Kaiser's consent. Concurrence would have automatically created a rift between Germany and Russia, and the Kaiser, reluctantly or not, blandly refused. Although he would later be reconciled to the courtship, Vicky's father at first opposed it, a fact confirmed by that inveterate matchmaker, Queen Victoria. Apart from detesting the Russians, she was genuinely anxious to effect the marriage. To her grand-daughter Victoria of Hesse, the matriarch wrote from Balmoral on 30 August 1883:

Tho' I wrote on Tuesday, I must write again – this time it is about Sandro. I think I told you at Osborne that Aunt Vicky feared Uncle Fritz wld. make gt. difficulties. But I don't think I told you that Aunt V wrote to me that Victoria (to whom the *possibility* of Sandro's *wishing* to marry *her* has *not* been told) is violently *in love* with Sandro; says she never cared for anyone else, or even *will* marry anyone else; – that she will wait any time for him & has refused to *look* at *any* other Princes who might be good *partis* for her. Uncle F was very angry & tried to put it out of her head – but he did not succeed & she is more than ever anxious abt. it. I got another letter from At. V this mng of wh. I send you an extract. Now cld. you, through Ludwig [Louis of Battenberg], manage to get Sandro *not* to *come forward now* – & let *him* know of V's feelings so as to induce him to wait, possibly it *might* come to pass.

This must be done *very confidentially* & *secretly*.

In September the following year she recorded that 'the Emperor and Empress are violently against it, and they are very unkind, and the Empress expecially won't look at or speak to the poor girl; and her brothers and sisters are also most unkind.'

Temporarily the romance would be eclipsed by more dramatic events. Under the Berlin Treaty, Eastern Rumelia – the southern region of Bulgaria – had remained a Turkish province. Discontent among the nationalists, however, festered into revolt at Philippopel on 18 September 1885. Sandro was not in Sofia when Major Nikolajev, commander-in-chief of the southern forces, informed him by telegram of the union. The people, moreover, had proclaimed Sandro their prince. According to the memoirs of his sister Marie, Sandro telegraphed the Tsar that, the union having been accomplished without his co-operation, nothing remained but to place himself at the head of the revolutionaries. That Ischitchakov and Igelstrom, the Russian representatives in Philippopel, had welcomed Sandro with enthusiasm rather implied that the Russian Government was sympathetic towards union. Tsarist reaction, however, was strikingly different. Russian officers were ordered to quit the Bulgarian army, and, like his father years earlier, Sandro was divested of Russian rank. To save the union, Sandro offered to withdraw, but Alexander III remained silent; neither he nor Bismarck wished to promote a Battenberg to martyrdom.

Threatened with attack from the Turks and the Serbs, Sandro summarized some of his anxieties in a letter, dated 13 November, to his parents.

The close connection between the Battenbergs and the Romanoffs weakened on the accession of Tsar Alexander III, seen here with the Empress Dagmar.

Prince Alexander of Battenberg ('Sandro'), the first Sovereign Prince of Bulgaria. He was crowned by his godfather, Alexander II, and ousted from his throne by Alexander III and Bismarck.

The 18th September [he revealed] threw me into the water . . . I wish all the statesmen who treat me so contemptuously in their official organs could be in my shoes for only a week . . . when one remembers with how many nationalities I have to contend, what rivalries I have to consider, and how every male inhabitant, be he child or man, is armed to the teeth, and that with them 'to murder' is synonymous with 'to hunt'; further, that I am compelled, owing to the small supplies at my disposal, to feed ninety thousand men by means of requisitions, and that officers and men receive no pay – further, that I have to tolerate in the country consuls who, unpunished, use their consular immunities to influence the people against me.

War with King Milan of Serbia was drawing closer. The Rumelian militia trained seven hours daily, learning more in six weeks than they had in the previous six years of their existence. Sandro reported that the arrangements for supply were excellent but that arms and clothing were inadequate, in spite of his energetic attempts to rectify the situation.

Due to his immaturity, Sandro doubtless had shortcomings in diplomacy, yet – like his ancestors – he was no novice in the art of war. He inflicted an ignominious defeat on the more professional Serbian army, from Slivnitza to Pirot. Koch, Sandro's Court chaplain, said of him:

If the battle were over, he rode among his troops to inspire them anew with courage and to fill them with anticipations of victory. At night, while the soldiers slept, he worked for the coming day. He shared hunger and cold with his troops, and slept, like them, on the cold ground.

At the same time the Prince took the greatest pains imaginable to organize the commissariat . . . the soldiers, notwithstanding the impending battle, got their food every day, so that, in contrast to the Serbian army, the Bulgarians had a superfluity of munitions. When Count Revenhüller [the Austro–Bulgarian ambassador in Belgrade] announced the cessation of hostilities, the already routed Serbs had only five cartridges per man . . . while the Prince, on the same day, had still eight million reserve cartridges at his disposal.

Slivnitza was Sandro's Bulgarian heyday. It drew praise from Queen Victoria, but it intensified tsarist hate. Through lies, deceit and bribes – and by enlisting the services of Zankoff, a disaffected ex-minister – the Russians sowed corruption, convincing many Bulgarians that their Sovereign Prince wished to return them to their former oppressors. In the European capitals baseless innuendoes accused Sandro of ruining Bulgaria, of keeping a harem, even of homosexual tendencies.

In his own words, Sandro was beset on all sides like a hunted stag – 'Of course all these evil ideas are the result of foreign promptings.' Francis Joseph of Battenberg, who had fought with his brother Sandro against the Serbs, informed Prince Louis: 'He has grown thin, and looks very strained. Sometimes he has melancholy moods, to which he is very prone. But he has a great deal to cope with; nothing but enemies, intrigues and deceit on all sides.'

Sandro's sister Marie recorded how the Russians tried to poison him. In the Court dispensary a chemist's assistant mixed a lethal poison with a Seidlitz powder, but Sandro, suspicious of the taste and smell, discarded it.

Agents were more successful at inflaming revolt. According to Sandro's own account, on 12 August 1886, having worked late into the night, he was awakened by a noise outside his room. 'The next minute Dimitri [his servant] rushed in, shaking and shivering, and crying: "You are betrayed, they want to kill you! Fly, before it is too late!" I sprang out of bed and seized my revolver. Then I heard the military word of command, and breathed again: "I am rescued – the military are there!" But Dimitri cried out in despair: "No, no, fly! It is the soldiers who want to kill you!"'

From outside the palace came the strident sound of rifle fire, and men were shouting 'Down with the Prince!' But escape was not to be thought of. 'I put out my light and in the darkness got into my uniform. I did not stop for socks or underwear ... The noise and clash of weapons grew louder.' In the corridor bayonets glinted in the light of a solitary candle. Sandro had no choice but to surrender. As insolent, drunken soldiers pushed him into the entrance-hall, his brother appeared; they had seized him too. In the confusion, someone ripped a leaf out of the visitors' book, and voices noisily demanded Sandro's abdication. When the leader menacingly raised his revolver, Sandro cried: 'Write yourself, and give me reason for my abdication. I know of none.' A bystander took the pen, but the erratic scrawl was meaningless to Sandro who, snatching the paper, wrote: 'God protect Bulgaria. Alexander.'

Then Sandro was taken to the War Ministry, where Captain Benderev, a commander in the Serbo-Bulgarian war, contemptuously informed him: 'You are going to Russia.' Then the brothers, hustled into separate carriages, were driven to the St Michael Monastery, some sixteen miles from the capital, where they were put into 'a narrow, stuffy room infested with bugs, fleas, and other noxious vermin'. There was neither table nor chair. In the morning they continued to Braza, which they reached at night-time. The next halt was at Rachova on the Danube, where the Bulgarian state yacht was lying. Taken downstream, the brothers were confined to the dining-room in stifling heat. Double sentries were posted at the doors and windows, which no one was allowed to open. The ship's engines had been over-heated to maintain high speed and to frustrate any contemplated rescue from the Roumanian bank of the river. None was made – fortunately, for the guards had orders to shoot Sandro at the first attempt.

Curiously, when the yacht moored at Reni on the Black Sea, the Russian authorities were embarrassed by the presence of the Battenberg Princes and ordered officials to escort them to the frontier. Sandro proposed to travel to Lemburg in Austrian Galicia, and the Russians arranged a special train for the Princes.

Louis, who had journeyed to Hesse on learning of his brothers' abduction, now hurried to Lemburg. Subsequently he wrote to Queen Victoria:

I have not yet got over the effect produced on me by the account of all that unparalleled baseness, duplicity & brutality ... I found S quite crushed and broken, longing to lay down his weary head far, far from the scene of all his suffering, sick to death of the mere word 'Bulgaria'. And it was then that his grand nature shewed itself again to the full. No sooner had he taken in the whole situation and had found that it was his *duty* to go back, as things had turned, than his resolve was taken ...

On her part, the Queen commented: 'What dreadful anxiety we have been living in since that awful 22nd! & those 3 days before we knew where dear noble brave Sandro was! When we heard his dear life was safe & the enthusiasm so great for him, & that wicked, villainous, atrocious Russia failed – I felt as if I cld have jumped for joy!'

If Russian intrigue had been foiled, it was only temporary. Blood had flowed in a counter-revolution led by Stefan Stambulov, the liberal leader, and a provisional government under Stambulov begged Sandro to return. But beneath the 'frantic delight of the populace', an undercurrent moved against him. The National Assembly, for instance, did not unanimously favour his restoration. And without consulting others of greater political wisdom, Sandro foolishly placed himself at Tsar Alexander's mercy, naïvely imagining that in so doing he would ingratiate himself into his cousin's good-will. 'I should be happy to give Your Majesty the final proof of the unchanging devotion which I feel for Your Majesty's illustrious person. As Russia gave me the crown, I am prepared to give it back into the hands of its Sovereign.' Sandro had blundered; the ingenuous Prince had trapped himself in his own net. As his desperate father later informed him: '. . . your last sentence was terribly dangerous, apart from the fact that it was contrary to the Treaty of Berlin ... You have cast your pearls before swine.'

The spiteful Tsar had no desire for rapport, and wrote to Sandro to say that he could not countenance his return to Bulgaria for fear of the disastrous results such a move would bring about.

Queen Victoria was furious and tried to obstruct Sandro's abdication, observing: 'My resentment and fury against your barbaric, asiatic-like tyrannical cousin is *so great* that I can hardly control myself to write about it ... If you want and can stay on ... you must ... appeal to the Great Powers (but not to Russia) ... Ever your loving cousin and true friend, Victoria RI.' A telegram from Prince Henry of Battenberg to Sandro indicated that the Queen considered the best solution to be open hostility to Russia. There was a fair amount of tinder but no fire. In the crisis, Queen Victoria's government made its protests, but Lord Salisbury, her Prime Minister, shrank from sending warships to the Bosphorus. In Prussia the Crown Princess urged her husband to plead with the Kaiser on Sandro's behalf. But Bismarck, whom she hated, delivered his typical *coup de grâce*. 'When Prince Battenberg', he wrote, 'became the ruler of Bulgaria in 1879, it was understood by all that he would attach himself and Bulgaria to Russia. As was to be expected from his character, which together with his qualities and faults he had inherited from his Polish rather than his German ancestry, he has given all the impression that no reliance can be placed either on his judgement or on his trustworthiness.'

The Battenberg pawn was no longer useful on the Balkan chessboard. With German

The revolt on the night of
12 August 1886. Soldiers
insolently demanded
Alexander's abdication.
Despite a counter-revolution,
he was compelled to quit.

Princess Victoria of Prussia.
She had hoped to marry
Alexander of Bulgaria but
politics and her brother,
Kaiser William II, prevented
it.

and Turkish support, Russia made it manifestly clear that, to avoid armed conflict in Bulgaria, the Prince must confirm 'the abdication he had already signed' – meaning the scrap of paper Sandro had signed at revolver-point on the night of the revolt. Sacrificing himself, humiliated, Sandro quit Bulgaria early in September. In the farewell scenes, people wept in the streets. The tears would flow again when his mortal remains were borne to Sofia seven years later.

Now deprived of his sovereign duties, Sandro expected to visit Cousin Vicky (who still affirmed her love for him) in Potsdam. Almost three years had passed since their last meeting. But Bismarck's implacable figure reared itself again. A visit was inopportune, Sandro was told; the Kaiser 'was at present unable to receive him'. Moreover, a visit would be misinterpreted in other capitals.

Sandro received a hero's welcome on his return to Darmstadt, but life was full of frustrations; the future was uncertain. At this period perhaps the most undermining aspect was his elusive courtship of Vicky, which was entangled with political barbs and the question of rank. Whereas the Crown Princess – and now the Crown Prince – with the articulate support of Queen Victoria, keenly favoured an official betrothal, the Kaiser William, the Empress Augusta and their grandson Prince William just as vehemently opposed it. And always lurking in the shadows was Bismarck's great bulk, ever ready to veto the courtship on political grounds. For young William, that overbearing Prince, the objection was twofold: as well as the political aspect, there was the question of equal birth. The Battenbergs, with their morganatic origin, could not be allowed to marry into the august house of Hohenzollern. Already the future Kaiser William II had quarrelled with his English mother. In 'a terrible row' the arrogant prince had raged: 'As usual, the Battenbergs cause trouble. Such a marriage would only result in a rift between Germany and Russia.' Furiously, he denounced the possibility of a Battenberg in his family.

Thus the courtship bred its controversies and fostered unhappiness. Conspiracy, quite unexpectedly, was another offshoot. Doubtless the most ardent champion of Sandro's interests was the Crown Princess herself, and, on 9 March 1888 – a day of bitter cold caused by a heavy snowfall – came her chance to end the impasse: the feeble old Kaiser William I died, less than a fortnight from his ninety-first birthday. Within the same month the new Empress Victoria had persuaded her husband to sanction their daughter's marriage to the Battenberg Prince. 'He gave me his consent personally at Potsdam,' wrote Vicky of her father, 'and how lovingly we embraced one another. I believe he planned to bring about the marriage there and then...' An invitation was extended to Sandro to visit Charlottenberg Palace in the next month. Yet for Vicky marital bliss, which now seemed so joyfully close, would be as tantalizingly evasive as ever. Her father's reign would last a mere ninety-two days. What had begun as an irritation of the throat had been diagnosed as cancer. The Kaiser Frederick was dying, and by now his communication with others was confined to scribbling notes on a writing-pad. It was his intention to confer on Sandro high military rank, but when he broached the subject on the last day of March, the Chancellor told him to choose between this proposal or his (Bismarck's) resignation. Only the minister's dismissal – a move from which Frederick shrank – could have made the marriage possible. (Ironically, nemesis would administer its own punishment in due course. William, the Kaiser's son, would end the Chancellor's tyranny after his father's death.)

The overpowering Bismarck even tried to thwart a visit of Queen Victoria to her dying son-in-law. Her Prime Minister, Lord Salisbury, warned that the visit might arouse the Chancellor's displeasure. But the formidable Queen was unmoved by the threat of Teutonic fury. More disconcerting was the astonishing report that she now received from Prince Henry of Battenberg. Sandro, it transpired, was no longer romantically inclined towards his cousin Vicky. His affections now centred on an Austrian, Johanna Loisinger, an opera singer at the Darmstadt Theatre. The despondent Queen withheld the news from her dying son-in-law at Charlottenberg, where Bismarck sought a meeting with the Queen. The gist of that confrontation is unrecorded; no other persons were present. But when the Chancellor emerged from the room, he was heard to say: 'What a woman. One could do business with her.'

The 'Battenberg Affair' was over, but Vicky's heart-break had not ended. Stifling her emotions, the disconsolate Princess now witnessed the preparations for the forth-coming wedding of her brother Henry to Princess Irene of Hesse. Added to this there was the despicable behaviour of her brother William. A poignant postscript occurred after her father's death on 15 June. With his testament, the Kaiser Frederick left a letter, dated 18 April, to his heir, by then the formidable Kaiser William II. It was clear that Frederick had categorically consented to the marriage of Victoria with the Battenberg Prince, for he instructed:

Should your mother or myself be suddenly called to depart this life, I hereby wish to state definitely that I give full consent to the marriage of your second sister Victoria with the ex-Prince of Bulgaria, Alexander of Battenberg. I charge you by the love you bear your father to carry out this my last wish, which has been the heart's desire of your sister Victoria for many years. To avoid any suggestion of politics and to obviate any political difficulties, I give up my wish to grant the Prince, to whom I am greatly attached, a position in my army or any official decoration. I count on you to fulfil your duty as my son by complying with my wish and trust that, as a brother, you will not refrain from helping your sister. Your loving father, Frederick William.

At this stage, considering his attachment to his opera singer, one cannot contemplate what Sandro's reaction might have been. He had already written sad farewell letters to Vicky and her mother, renouncing 'the dreams of my youth'. To Johanna Loisinger he had confided: 'Behind locked doors I have allowed my tears to flow without being able to prevent it; they were for the grave of my youthful dreams, the collapse of all I had striven and hoped for many years, the failure of all my political and military plans.' Whether he would have recanted, one cannot say, but the new Kaiser dashed

53

all hopes of a revived courtship. This contemptible monarch, who cruelly tried to debase whatever high standards his parents had symbolized, callously ignored the wish of his dying father.

Years later Princess Victoria of Hesse (then the Marchioness of Milford Haven) recalled: 'Unfortunately ... in the high and mighty Hohenzollern fashion, William sent the British diplomatic representative to my father-in-law [Prince Alexander of Hesse] to announce that all question of a marriage must be at an end, as the Emperor would never countenance it. My poor father-in-law was furious at the impertinence of such a message being delivered to him, as he had never asked for the hand of a Prussian princess for one of his sons.' Sandro's letter from the Kaiser did not refer to the engagement; he was therefore not held to break it in the desired manner. Queen Victoria was equally indignant.

The intrigues surrounding the contemplated marriage had seeped like poison into Battenberg life. This and the anxieties bred by the Bulgarian nightmare no doubt eroded the health of Prince Alexander of Hesse. In August 1888 Sandro accompanied him to Bayreuth, then he visited his last surviving cousin, the Duchess Ludovika of Bavaria, in Munich. It was on his return to Heiligenberg that a digestive complaint was diagnosed as cancer. Neither he nor Princess Julie was ever told the truth; he had only three more months to live.

Whether Alexander suspected the approach of death is not known, but (according to his daughter Marie) he alluded to his suffering with the remark: 'I have a vampire in me which is devouring me.' With Princess Julie, he travelled to Darmstadt in October, there devoting hours to the study of coins. By Advent, Alexander was weakening and was virtually confined to his bed. There he listened to Marie reading his favourite passages from the scriptures – the Psalms and extracts from St John's Gospel – which pleased him. He would be grateful that circumstances enabled him to meet all his family together before he died. Even Louis, who now had a command in the Mediterranean, journeyed to Darmstadt, and after a family observance of Holy Communion, Alexander gave his blessing to each, beginning with Princess Julie.

Marie described a strange incident in her father's final days:

... It was toward evening – I was sitting alone by his bedside; he lay still and motionless; suddenly he half-raised himself, with his eyes, large and questioning, directed to a spot on the wall opposite. I asked him gently: 'What is the matter, papa, do you see anything?' Slowly he pointed upwards with his hand, and whispered, 'My sister tells me she is there' – I listened breathlessly – 'and she says she is happy, and that I, too, shall be happy.' An expression of deep peace came over his face as he sank back on his pillows.

Deeply moved, I went into the next room. There I found my cousin the Grand Duke Sergius, and his wife, the Grand Duchess Ella, who were on a visit to her father, the Grand Duke Ludwig IV. Sergius, who was very fond of my father, had spent a short time with him every day.

In a voice choked with tears, I told him what had just occurred. He fell on his knees and, raising his folded hands to heaven, cried, 'Oh! my God! I thank Thee Thou hast heard my prayer!' And then he told me that for long he had prayed every day that his mother might be allowed to appear to her dying brother, to comfort him and to ease his departure.

Alexander of Hesse, the confidant of emperors and kings, whose life had long been entwined with Europe's politics, died on 15 December 1888. For two years his body remained temporarily in the Rosenhöhe, the grand ducal mausoleum where Princess Julie sometimes sat for hours beside the coffin. Broken in mind and body, her health in a precarious state, the Princess retired into a deaconess house. Gradually, with her family's aid, her resilience enabled her to return to Heiligenberg, where she lived with her memories. But shocks still intruded into her serene widowhood. Her nerves were gravely undermined when a mosquito-curtain caught alight and spread a serious fire at Heiligenberg. A similar but more disastrous mishap at the castle of Schönberg, seven years after her husband's death, had a lamentable outcome; Princess Julie returned to Darmstadt and died suddenly some days later.

The coffins of Alexander and Julie, the co-founders of the Battenbergs and Mount-battens, were placed side by side in the Kreuzgarten at Heiligenberg. Nearby, like a gnarled old link with past centuries, stands the 'Cent Linden' tree, where the Court of the Hundred was held in the time of Charlemagne, Alexander's remote ancestor. There, overshadowed by fir trees, Alexander and Julie lie 'united in time and eternity' beneath a simple white tombstone designed in 1901 by the Empress Frederick, herself then dying of cancer.

Seven weeks after his father's death, Sandro left Darmstadt. Sadly, Princess Julie never saw her son again. Trying to shed his past, with the Grand Duke's permission he sacrificed his princely status, taking instead the title 'Count von Hartenau', after a village near Battenberg. As had his father years earlier, Sandro applied to serve the Austrian Emperor, moving to Vienna when Francis Joseph offered him the colonelship of an infantry regiment. The appointment was, however, delayed by tragedy – a notorious drama that might have embarrassed Sandro. On 28 January 1889 Archduke Rudolf, the Austrian Crown Prince, whom Sandro had known since childhood, invited him to stay at his hunting lodge at Mayerling. Sandro declined, giving as his reason a proposed visit to Venice – fortunately for him, for within days Rudolf and Baroness Marie Vetsera, his young mistress, were found dead with gunshot wounds.

On 6 February 1889, without warning his family, Sandro married Johanna Loisinger in Mentone. The simple ceremony had an electrifying effect on the courts of Europe, from which Sandro was now debarred. 'Oh! dear Sandro,' wrote Queen Victoria, 'it is a sad thing – especially that he did it without saying one word to any one of his brothers & in such a hurry!' Princess Julie had observed that she would 'never consent to such a disastrous match', but time would prove that it was not a calamitous union. Indeed, now free from dynastic intrigue, Sandro at last achieved consummate happiness in the four years that remained to him.

Like an echo from the distant past, he settled down to garrison life in Graz, the town which had been his parents' sanctuary after their marriage. For Sandro and his wife the future was financially secure. Apart from his army pay, in Bulgaria the faithful Stambulov secured for Sandro an annual pension of 50,000 gold francs, and the sale of Sandro's possessions in Bulgaria are said to have realized two million *levas*.

As if to renew a link with the past, when his son was born on 16 January 1890, Sandro christened him Assen after a Bulgarian hero. It is significant, too, that, during the spring of 1893, when Sandro met his sister Marie in Florence, he startled her by making her promise that, if the Bulgarians would permit it, he would be buried in Sofia. Marie stared at him in amazement, but her consternation could not weaken her brother's resolve. Visiting Venice together some days later, she last saw him in a gondola waving farewell. Six months later she was called upon to fulfil that promise. On 16 November while she was at König, a telegram warned her that Sandro was dangerously ill. The next day, accompanied by her husband Gustav, she set out for Graz. But Sandro was beyond aid. A telegram bearing news of Sandro's death reached her at the station at Würzburg. She later described her feelings: 'As if stunned, I continued the journey all night long; in Vienna, in the morning, mourning had to be obtained. I stood silently by. At last, towards evening, we came to Graz ...'

Marie did not see Sandro's body at the Hartenau villa.

In front of a door [she later explained] hung with black, stood two '*Leichenbitter*' – it was a 'first-class' funeral. 'Beg pardon, the coffin is already closed – the corpse is no longer to be seen.' I was pushed into an immense sky-blue apartment. Sandro's widow lay in bed ... I had only seen her hitherto on the stage. I took her in my arms. I spent the evening with her. She accepted the long-refused nourishment. From her and others I had the story of the last days.

Appendicitis – an operation no longer possible – a painful death ... It was the anniversary of Slivnitza – Sandro was aware of it – delirium set in – he thought he was on the battlefield, gave the word of command – and died! 'Victory – victory!' were his last words.

Marie's dilemma was to honour her pledge of the previous April, for plans were already afoot to inter Sandro in the Graz burial-ground three days after his death, as was the custom. Time was pressing. Without waiting for the arrival of her brothers, she telegraphed Stambulov, referring to the promise Sandro had extracted in Florence. Moments of frustration were eased by the unexpected arrival of the Infante Alfonso of Spain, an exile in Graz, who had known Sandro well. To help Marie, he secured a provisional resting-place for his former friend – a newly-built mausoleum owned by a Herr Reinighaus – and Marie convinced the Countess that a chapel was more desirable temporarily than a grave.

On 20 November – three days after his death – Sandro's remains were placed in the Reinighaus chapel with much pomp. Marie, who had learned that Bulgaria desired the return of its first Prince, was visited by Bulgarian ministers at her hotel. Grecoff,

Minister for the Affairs of the External Greeks at Graz, explained that the body of His Highness was to be removed in two days' time. The Countess was totally ignorant of the plan and had already retired to her bed when Marie returned with the ministers to tell her of it.

I felt like an executioner [she subsequently recorded] as I sat down by the bedside of the poor woman, in order to inform her ... of the cruel fact that the removal of the body was contemplated. It was a frightful scene which now ensued. I remained firm and explained that it was my sacred duty to fulfil my promise to Sandro, and tried to make it clear that it was no longer Count Hartenau who had been interred in Graz, but the first Prince of Bulgaria, whom his people desired to have back. Gradually she calmed down ... and in the end consented.

On 25 November a special train bearing Sandro's remains left Graz for Sofia. Near the heights of Slivnitza, it was greeted by the thunder of guns. Later, on leaving the cathedral in Sandro's former capital, his body was temporarily buried in the old church of St George, until a marble mausoleum was erected in Sofia. Stambulov, who had delivered an oration at the funeral, was himself dead two years later – murdered because, like Sandro, he could not reconcile himself with Russian domination.

Queen Victoria, on learning of Sandro's marriage, had merely observed: 'Perhaps they love one another.' On his arrival at Graz, Louis informed her:

I reached here, after many delays owing to snowfalls, towards two o'clock this morning. My poor sister-in-law was sitting up for me. I was aghast at the change in her appearance. She, who I last saw as a tall, fine woman, is shrunk to nothing ... a thin, frail white-faced girl ... She led me in silence to Sandro's room ... I believe I realized for the first time that he was in truth gone. I completely and utterly broke down ... She stood there all the time, not a tear in her eye, not a sound escaped her ...

Had cousin Vicky also stifled her tears? And had she never ceased to adore Sandro? Among the Communion vessels in the memorial chapel at Heiligenberg, there stands a golden chalice in which Vicky's mother, the Empress Frederick, had set all the jewels which Sandro had given to his intended bride. Princess Victoria retained only one, a sapphire ring, and at the very hour of Sandro's death this stone was cracked. Interpreting the mishap as a portent, she felt impelled to visit Princess Julie, from whom she learned the sad news.

Vicky found some solace in marrying the sympathetic Adolphus, Prince of Schaumburg-Lippe, in 1891. After his death in 1916, she surprised Europe by her eccentricities. At the age of sixty she married a Russian commoner of twenty-seven, Alexander Zubkov, an ex-waiter, who gradually deprived her of her fortune. For years this peculiar union was the subject of lurid headlines, until it foundered and Zubkov finally went to gaol. Her death in 1929 was unexpected; some suspected that she took her own life.

5

Scandal and Romance

DURING 1879 Prince Louis of Battenberg, then serving in the *Agincourt*, yielded yet again to royal persuasion, spending six months in the royal yacht *Osborne*, which Prince Arthur, Duke of Connaught, was using for his Mediterranean honeymoon. However, it was not the cruise which earns mention but the ship's commander. Louis had first met Lord Charles Beresford – the eccentric son of a marquess, with fiery Irish charm – when the latter was the Prince of Wales's aide-de-camp on the India tour. They would never be intimates – Beresford's turn of mind was never to Prince Louis's liking – but their paths would cross over the years, ending in an acrimonious climax in the First World War. Meanwhile, when the *Osborne* went into dock to be overhauled, Louis, to the Prince of Wales's delight, found himself without a ship.

The social round was renewed, interspersed with journeys to the Continent and Russia. From the latter Louis returned to London in March 1880 to what he believed to be a true romance; he was attracted – passionately and unashamedly, so it seems – to the person whom many regarded as the most enchanting woman in London society, Lillie Langtry. Her husband, a rogue, had long since vanished from the marital scene, to be replaced by many admirers, among whom was the Prince of Wales himself. Indeed, so discreet was the liaison between Louis and the actress that the Prince – rather than Louis – was widely held to be her lover during this period. Yet no one could have been mistaken after a notorious party given by Lord and Lady Randolph Churchill, at which, spurred on by the effects of champagne, the 'Jersey Lily', as she was known, tactlessly slipped a piece of ice down the Prince's back. 'Bertie' was not amused, quitting the party in a rage, and Lillie was spontaneously shunned by society. Thus ostracized, her circle of actors, artists and writers had induced her to return to the stage that autumn, until she realized she was expecting a child.

When Prince Louis told his parents of his indiscretion, Prince Alexander squashed the romance with alacrity, sending an aide-de-camp from Heiligenberg to conclude the affair with a financial settlement. With consummate care Lillie Langtry protected the Battenbergs from the slightest scandal, yet this imprudent episode in Louis's life was exposed in a London stage production in April 1940.

Fortunately for Louis, a world cruise in the *Inconstant*, the flagship of a squadron of five men-of-war, took him away from the distractions of the 'Marlborough set' and the frivolous London scene. Louis learned much about seamanship during the cruise, but more important was the lifelong bond created with the future King George V. As midshipmen young George and his elder brother Eddie, the sons of the Prince of Wales, were raw recruits in one of the four accompanying corvettes, the *Bacchante*.

The squadron had sailed down the east coast of South America and crossed to the Falkland Islands, when the Admiralty urgently ordered it to proceed to South Africa where a revolution had broken out among the Boers. But by the time the ships anchored in Simon's Bay, the British force had been defeated at Majuba Hill. This was regrettable considering that the naval brigade of one thousand men and eight guns would most probably have ensured a British victory and warded off the Boer War almost two decades later.

But for the emergency, the squadron would have voyaged round Cape Horn, but now it was instructed to visit Australia and Japan, a decision that – due to a violent storm – almost resulted in disaster. In an account of that agonizing experience, Louis wrote:

I had the middle watch. Steering became extremely difficult. The seas were parallel hills and vales, stretching to right and left as far as the eye could reach. They were so far apart that this long ship could run down one side and up the other, just keeping ahead of the seas which were continuously breaking astern of us. The sky was perfectly clear, with full moon and all the stars out. The foam of the wave crests was continually being spread by the wind like snow on the surface of the water which shone white under the moon.

We rolled so heavily that the quarter boats [cutters] were dipped repeatedly, whilst the whalers hoisted at the same long, straight davits inside the cutters, were flattened out like the cocked hat carried by diplomats at Court, under the arm. I spent the four hours clinging to the standard compass and watching it and the double-manned steering wheel just below.

As the gale abated, three of the other ships were sighted, but not the *Bacchante*. The anxiety was now intense. For the moment it was not known that during the night, at the height of the storm, the fierce seas had wrenched off her rudderhead and the *Bacchante* almost breached to and swamped. At the crucial moment, the commander had got the ship before the wind in time, ordering the watch into the fore-rigging, the wind pressure on the men's bodies gradually forcing the ship's head to leeward. If the *Bacchante* had got into the trough of the sea, she would have been swamped and lost, and with her the two young Princes.

On the evening of 20 May 1881, the *Inconstant* sighted Cape Otway near Melbourne where the lighthouse men conveyed the message: '*Bacchante* at Albany.' The Princes were saved. Everyone on board, officers as well as men, shouted themselves hoarse in their relief.

In Australia the major interest appears to have centred on Prince Louis's good looks, one newspaper commenting: '. . . he looks born to "kill" at any distance within eye-shot.'

Prince Louis wrote prolifically on his experiences in the Fiji Islands, Japan, the Chinese Treaty ports and Hong Kong. From there, in February 1882, accompanied by two of the corvettes, the *Inconstant* left for Singapore, the Cape of Good Hope, St Helena and the Cape Verde Islands. Here the squadron was ordered to proceed with all despatch to Gibraltar to collaborate with a reserve fleet in suppressing the Arab insurrection in Egypt. The main task was to protect British nationals and interests, including the Suez Canal.

The *Inconstant* arrived too late to participate in the bombardment of Alexandria but undertook other duties. Prince Louis was ordered to take six Gatling guns and a detachment of bluejackets to guard the Khedive, who was expected at Ras-el-Tin from Ramleh. With Boyce, his servant, and Mark Kerr, a midshipman,

We spent an uncomfortable night in an empty transport alongside Gabari Docks. Early the next morning I marched my small army off ... At Ras-el-Tin we found half a battalion of the Berkshire Regiment (49th) installed in a wing of the Palace. I was given two very dirty bare rooms, which had apparently been the humbler quarters of the Khedive's harem. The Palace was large and straggling, and quite deserted except the inner part, occupied by His Highness, but we soon looted enough gilt and silk-covered furniture to make ourselves comfortable, after scrubbing out and white-washing the place. I procured two horses for Mark and myself from the Khedive's bodyguard ... Mark looted some excellent liqueurs out of the cellar of a deserted house in the town ...'

At the end of a fortnight Louis's 'picnic' at Ras-el-Tin ended abruptly. The *Inconstant* re-embarked, anchoring at Spithead on 16 October 1882. At Marlborough House 'Uncle Bertie and Aunt Alix received me like a lost son,' wrote Louis. Soon he was caught up once more in the Waleses' social world, but Hesse was also beckoning: almost two years had elapsed since he had last seen his family. He also planned to visit Sandro in Sofia.

On returning from Bulgaria, Prince Louis had become engaged to his cousin Victoria, the daughter of Louis IV, Grand Duke of Hesse. She was nineteen, of resolute mind and, despite her age, possessed a confident poise derived partly from serving as her father's hostess for five years. Her mother, Princess Alice, had died during a domestic crisis in November 1878. It had begun on that winter's night when Victoria, after reading aloud *Alice in Wonderland* to the younger children, had complained of a sore throat which was soon diagnosed as diphtheria. The disease, from which Ella would be the only member of the Grand Duke's family to escape, was highly pernicious that year. Thus, aided by eight doctors and nurses, Princess Alice slept little, nursing her husband and children day after day.

'My precious May no better,' she telegraphed to Queen Victoria on 15 November. 'Suffers so much. I am in such horrible fear. Irene and Ernie fever less. Ernie's throat very swelled.' The following day, forty-eight hours after the Grand Duke himself was

Princess Victoria of Hesse, Queen Victoria's favourite grandchild, who married Prince Louis of Battenberg, thus strengthening the bond between the Battenbergs and the British royal family.

Prince Henry of Battenberg, whose marriage to Princess Beatrice, Victoria's shyest and most devoted daughter meant that the Battenbergs, had passed into the line of Queen Victoria's children. The Prince became a close confidant of the monarch.

stricken, the four-year-old May died. It was a blow from which Alice never recovered. On 7 December, after greeting her sister-in-law Marie, Duchess of Edinburgh, at Darmstadt Station, Alice also succumbed. But her constitution had long been under-mined. She had, indeed, complained of ill-health to Queen Victoria for some two years. Now, physically exhausted after weeks of sleepless strain, Alice, suffering acutely, could not withstand the infection. 'She will never have the strength to get through it,' predicted the Queen with awesome reality. On the morning of 14 December, at half past eight, she awoke for a while and was heard to say: 'From Friday to Saturday – four weeks – May – dear Papa . . .' Then, released from her suffering, she died. Precisely four weeks earlier little May had died; exactly seventeen years before, to the day, Prince Albert, whom Alice had nursed devotedly, lay dead. Years later, Victoria, writing of her mother's death, would observe: 'My childhood ended with her death, for I became the eldest and most responsible.'

Accounts of the Grand Duke's reactions to Louis's affection for his daughter are inconsistent. It can be argued that, for the time being at least, her primary duty had been towards her father. But now, for Victoria to marry a mere Serene Highness was, according to Hessian standards, no outstanding match. Indeed, it was made blatantly apparent that the Hessian Parliament would decline to grant the couple any form of financial award in the event of their marriage. The Prussian Hohenzollerns and the Russian Romanoffs were certainly critical, as were many of the minor royalties of Europe, who foolishly refused to dismiss the 'social taint' of the morganatic Battenbergs.

As for Princess Victoria, she appears to have been indifferent to criticism. There was much of the egalitarian in her; she was unimpressed by rank. Moreover, she had the support of the matriarch at Windsor. Corresponding with her grand-daughter, Queen Victoria wrote: 'I think that you have done well to choose only a Husband who is *quite* of your way of thinking & who in many respects is as English as you are – whose interests must be the same as yours & who dear Mama liked.' Some months later the Queen advised Victoria to be 'a steady good wife & *not* run after amusements, but find your happiness chiefly in your own home. Beware of London and M. Hse [Marlborough House]', referring disapprovingly to her licentious heir.

Virtually the whole of the British royal family and many of the royalties of Europe attended the wedding in Darmstadt on 30 April 1884 – a glittering event which was marred by an extraordinary indiscretion.

For some while now, the Grand Duke of Hesse had been involved in a liaison with Madame Alexandrine de Kolemine, the wife of Russia's chargé d'affaires in Darmstadt. Embarrassing complexities, it seemed, had been tactfully removed after her husband left Hesse and arranged a divorce. Although Princess Victoria and her brother and sisters were reconciled to Madame's presence at Court as their father's mistress, it was generally accepted that a morganatic marriage to a divorcée – who did not rise even to the rank of countess – would be intolerable. The Grand Duke fatuously thought otherwise. Gradually it was whispered about the Court that Louis IV proposed to make Madame de Kolemine his wife – rumours that hardened into fact when he acquainted his astonished children of his intentions. The secret was also confided to Prince Louis of Battenberg and a select coterie; other than this, no one was aware of the Grand Duke's proposals, including Queen Victoria.

Queen Victoria remained in complete ignorance, even when her son-in-law greeted her at Darmstadt Station with an exuberance that she regarded as indelicate for one in widowhood. But his high spirits would soon be quelled. There was a sense of outrage as the scandal leaked out. Prince Alexander of Hesse wrote: 'A terrible prospect. The Grand Duke seems to have lost his head completely ... The Queen has no idea of it, and for the present no one dares tell her.' Sir Henry Ponsonby, her Private Secretary, explained why: 'The Grand Duke had behaved badly', he wrote later, 'in not telling the Queen before she came to Darmstadt, because it places her in a most awkward position. If she goes away, it will create a scandal, if she remains it will look as if she approved the marriage.'

Five days before the wedding of Louis and Victoria, 'the painful communication' was made to the Queen. She was appalled but told Victoria: 'If dear Papa should feel lonely when you 3 elder are married – I should say nothing (tho it must pain me) if he chose to make a morganatic marriage with some nice, quiet, sensible & amiable person – who would at any rate command the respect of us all as of his Country.'

The situation was still confusingly vague on the day of the wedding, but anxiety turned into fury when the truth emerged. As Ponsonby observed later, after the wedding of Louis and Victoria the news came like a thunderclap – 'the Grand Duke married Madame Alexandrine de Kolemine the same evening.'

Queen Victoria's reaction was swift and merciless; she instructed the Prince of Wales to inform the Grand Duke and Madame de Kolemine that their marriage must be annulled at once. Louis IV could do nothing but obey; he had recklessly violated the royal code from which there was no reprieve. Moreover, the 'glory of the Hessian Court' was, as explained by Ponsonby, 'its alliance with other great ones'. The Grand Duke was isolated. Those who normally frowned on the morganatic Battenbergs could scarcely condone a marriage to a commonplace divorcée. The Hohenzollerns hastily left the 'contaminated Court'. Others did likewise, giving spurious excuses for their sudden departure. The British, however, adhered unflinchingly to their original plan. Ponsonby told the Queen's entourage that there would be no hurry – '... we go as settled on Monday. And we trust nothing will become public until we are well away.'

When approached by the Prince of Wales, Madame de Kolemine had been hysterical. She returned to Moscow, taking with her the unhappy Grand Duke's love letters, and threatening blackmail. Why her threats of blackmail fizzled out, one can only surmise. The pressures were doubtless too immense. Yet she did profit. An alleviating balm to personal pride – and perhaps abortive scheming – was the granting of a title and a substantial annuity, which she continued to receive even when she married another Russian diplomat, M. de Bacharacht.

On leaving the disconsolate Grand Duke in Darmstadt, Queen Victoria, to her chagrin, soon had a second romance to grapple with, and one which would affect her more closely. Beatrice, her shy, unmarried daughter, whom the matriarch was determined should remain a spinster, had fallen in love. Victoria's bashful child, who became almost speechless in the presence of someone unfamiliar to her, had arrived, by the time they bade farewell in Hesse, at a clandestine arrangement with Prince Henry of Battenberg. 'Liko', then twenty-six, more than a year younger than the plump Beatrice, ardently reciprocated her affection. It was a speedy romance, burgeoning in less than three weeks.

Away from the unsettling atmosphere of Darmstadt, Beatrice mustered the courage to seek her mother's sanction to marriage on returning to Windsor. Although outwardly selfish, Queen Victoria's reaction was to be expected. The Queen had grown to depend on her daughter, as she stressed when, on medical advice, in the summer of 1883, Beatrice had travelled to Aix-les-Bains to be treated for rheumatism. Hitherto mother and daughter had been separated for only a matter of days. 'Beatrice's absence is very grievous and unpleasant,' wrote the Queen to the Empress Augusta, 'and increases my depression & the ever-growing feeling of emptiness and bereavement, which nothing can ever really remove.'

The death of John Brown, the Queen's Scottish gillie, had added to Princess Beatrice's burden, for the Queen had become accustomed to his attentions. The onus was great, for Brown, despite his brusqueness – even arrant rudeness – had been invaluable. Beatrice had accepted Brown's behaviour with some restraint. Indeed, she had been brought up to accept it – but not so the Prince of Wales and the Duke of Edinburgh. Both abhorred Brown, who at times caused domestic rancour. Once, for instance, after an argument, the Queen summoned Affie and her Scottish gillie to appear before her. Affie asked for a witness, observing: 'If I see a man on board my ship on any subject, it is always in the presence of an officer.' Answering with some asperity, the Queen replied: 'This is not a ship, and I won't have naval discipline introduced here.' So intense was the dislike of the Prince of Wales for Brown that on his mother's death he is reputed to have personally broken a collection of plaster statuettes of the gillie discovered at Osborne.

Learning of her daughter's wish to marry Liko, the matriarch by all accounts told Princess Beatrice that she was 'just a silly gel', infatuated by the Battenberg Prince and, as she would discover in due course, it was merely a temporary foolish passion. The Queen had definite plans that 'Benjamina' should be her buttress in her old age.

Queen Victoria did not merely express resentment to the marriage; from that time her behaviour was mysterious. On the surface, her manner smacked of the sadistic, the lowering of a curtain of silence between herself and her unhappy daughter that persisted throughout most of the summer of 1884. It was a ridiculous situation. The Princess gave her mother the daily companionship which she demanded, yet communication was confined to scribbled notes pushed across the table by the Queen as they took meals together. Significantly, Beatrice ceased to be mentioned in the Queen's *Journal* and, with one exception – a postscript to a letter of condolence sent by the Queen to Lady Ampthill – in her copious correspondence.

From June to December of that year Beatrice might have been non-existent as far as her mother was concerned. Accounts of the Princess's reaction to her mother's folly are conflicting. We are presented on one hand with a picture of filial defiance to a degree that pleased many at Court, who considered that her chance of marriage should not be impeded. Against this, one is asked to visualize a crestfallen daughter, dejected and ignored in the Queen's apartments, weeping in her bed at night. One assumes that she laboured under a sense of injustice – a state of mind which was heightened by the fact that Beatrice's romantic experiences had been nil. In spite of her sharp intellect, her knowledge of life was pathetically slight. She had even recoiled at the sight of corsets displayed for sale while driving through Windsor, for she had not realized such things were sold in shops.

The matriarch did not have any personal objection to Prince Henry of Battenberg, but the idea that 'my dear little Benjamina will never marry but always stay with me' was deeply ingrained. Like his brother Sandro, Liko had been educated at the exclusive Schnepfental School – an establishment noted for its strict but progressive training – then entered the Dresden military college as a cadet. Before the gap widened between the Battenbergs and Bismarck, the German Kaiser granted him a commission in the élite *Gardes du Corps*.

Prince Alexander of Hesse and Princess Julie favoured the match between Liko and Beatrice, for such a union promised great dynastic significance – far in excess of the marriage of Princess Alice to Prince Louis of Hesse. True or not, Paris journals insinuated that Prince Henry had enlisted the services of Madame Lacroix, a lady notorious for seeking affluent brides – among them American heiresses – for princelings of slender means. But it is probably more likely that the well-groomed young guards officer had shown no haste to marry, for Berlin offered ample scope for a gay social life and an opportunity to indulge his love of sports: shooting, mountaineering and skating.

Now, only the Queen's perversity prevented their happiness. Gradually the royal obstinacy wilted before criticism. The Prince of Wales remonstrated with his mother, accusing her of being 'entirely selfish and intolerable'. Much more discreet overtures were made by the Crown Princess Frederick, the Grand Duke of Hesse and Prince Louis of Battenberg, now her grandson by marriage. Remarking that he loved and admired Beatrice as if she were his sister, Louis delighted the matriarch by disclosing that the Queen was to become a great-grandmother.

Liko was invited to stay at Kent House, Osborne, during Christmas. To his father, he wrote: 'The Queen is most gracious and kind. You can't think what a pleasant difference there is between the people of the Court here and in Germany ... one feels at home at once.'

Victoria was clearly impressed with her prospective son-in-law, and finally yielded, stipulating one condition: after the marriage Beatrice and Liko (who was to become a naturalized Briton with an army commission) should live with her. She adamantly refused to part with her mainstay. 'Of course it remains a shock to me,' she wrote to her grand-daughter Victoria, 'and there will be things very difficult to get over with my feelings – still as he is so amiable & prepared to do what I wish – I hope all may be for the best & may turn out well. Of course I *can't* spare Auntie, & especially at first they must *not* think of travelling or paying visits.'

Writing to Prince Alexander from Sofia, Sandro observed: 'Liko's engagement to Beatrice is of incalculable value. How the youngster managed to make Beatrice fall in love with him is a puzzle to me; for it must be admitted that Liko is not on a level with her intellectually. Of course I noticed in the spring that they were making eyes at one another, but I did not take it seriously, as I should never have thought that the Queen would agree ... How strange the fate of our family is! I wonder how it will all end.' Commenting on his own aspirations to marry his cousin Vicky of Prussia, he went on: 'The Crown Princess has sent me a most kindly letter and Vicky a heavy gold ring as a token of her love. Louis wrote and told me the Crown Princess had recently said to him the best thing would be if I would abdicate [as Prince of Bulgaria] and marry Vicky. I telegraphed to Louis at once that I would do so with the greatest possible pleasure if I could get Vicky. Now, if Liko married Beatrice, the German Emperor will give way too.'

The jubilation in Heiligenberg was not echoed in Britain. Many Britons received the announcement of the betrothal with disapproval. 'Are there no eligible bridegrooms in Britain?' they asked. First, they argued, Princess Victoria had gone to Prussia to be harassed by divided loyalties caused by war. Next, Princess Alice had left for Hesse, witnessing the savagery of Prussian militarism and meeting with an early death at thirty-five. There had been the marriage of Princess Helena to a German princeling, and the matriarch's sons had chosen brides in Germany, Denmark and Russia. Only Princess Louise had taken a Briton as bridegroom – the Marquess of Lorne. In the circumstances, was it not reasonable to expect the last of the Queen's unmarried children to do likewise?

This prejudice against Germans had originated with the Hanoverian dynasty's becoming Britain's rulers in 1714, when one contemporary writer observed: 'A flight of hungry Hanoverians, like so many famished vultures, fell with keen eye and bended talons on the fruitful soil of England.' Enmity towards German influence was summed up in Thackeray's comment: 'The German women plundered, the German secretaries plundered, the German cooks and attendants plundered; even Mustapha and Mahomet, the German Negroes, had a share in the booty.' Almost two centuries later, twelve years after the marriage of Liko and Beatrice, one citizen remarked: 'Will any flunky in Christendom tell one good thing that the Queen, her sons and daughters or any of her inexhaustible brood of pauper relations "made in Germany" has ever done for the people of this land? . . .'

When Parliament met to approve Princess Beatrice's annuity, at the time of her marriage, the Liberal republican Henry Labouchere, together with a number of anti-royalist Irish members, unsuccessfully opposed it. The engagement of Liko and Beatrice was also the subject of ill-founded gossip among minor royalty on the Paris boulevards but, as was to be expected, the greatest outcry of disapproval came from Prussia. Both Bismarck and the Hohenzollerns railed against Battenberg social advancement. The Prussian Chancellor swore to ruin 'this new Battenberg intrigue'. Bismarck's attitude was almost paranoiac. He had seen in Prince Louis's marriage to Princess Victoria of Hesse 'a move in Queen Victoria's subterranean plot against Germany'. The matriarch's verbal support for Sandro in Bulgaria had stimulated this opposition. Hence the claim that Liko's betrothal was 'another move in London's finely woven plot to drive a wedge between Germany and Russia'. He appealed to the Tsar to obstruct 'yet another dangerous political Battenberg marriage'.

Hohenzollern enmity was not unanticipated. The Prussian royal house had been incensed by the marriage of Princess Louise to Lord Lorne, who had calmly told the Queen: 'Ma'am, my ancestors were kings when the Hohenzollerns were *parvenus*.' Queen Victoria was annoyed by the offensive replies from Berlin. She had expected the Empress Augusta to convey delight that she would not be deprived of Beatrice's companionship. Yet the worst blow to the Queen's feelings was directed by the Crown Prince Frederick, for whom she had affection. To the Hohenzollerns, social rank eclipsed everything – even friendship and happiness. If the betrothal really matured into marriage, Frederick would have Liko as a brother-in-law. Hohenzollern snobbery found this incompatible: a mere Battenberg Serene Highness was much too lowly a relative for a future German Kaiser. Frederick referred to Liko's 'stock', Queen Victoria stressed, as if he was referring to animals.

The arrogant reactions of the Hohenzollerns inspired harsh words from Queen Victoria; she described them as 'foolish', 'insolent' and 'unamiable' (strong terms in the royal vocabulary), and concentrated her invective on William – 'That very foolish, undutiful and, I must add, unfeeling boy'. She described Prince William's wife, 'Dona', as a 'poor little insignificant pcess', and as to his brother-in-law, according to Victoria, he and his brothers and sisters were 'the children of a Fräulein von Geyersberg, a very bad woman, and they had been acknowledged by the whole of Europe as Princes of Baden'. The Queen struck an even more discordant note by stressing that, if one searched, one would find black sheep in the genealogy of most of the dynastic Houses of Europe. Quoting Lord Grenville, she observed: 'If the Queen of England chooses a person good enough for her daughter, what have other people got to say?' Innuendo in Germany set free the ridiculous rumour that the Queen wished to relax the question of rank so that she could marry someone much lower in status than herself. Indeed, Duke Ernest of Coburg, the dead consort's brother, who Victoria now shunned due to his criticism of John Brown, disseminated an absurd account that she designed to marry a Scotsman.

Opposition to the betrothal of Beatrice and Liko dwindled before Victoria's castigation. But the antagonism to the Battenbergs was only dormant, awakening again when Beatrice's daughter Ena married the King of Spain.

The upshot of the criticism was that the wedding, on 23 July 1885, was celebrated somewhat quietly at Whippingham on the Isle of Wight. The Queen viewed the approach of the ceremony with some trepidation. 'I am *very depressed*,' she wrote to her grand-daughter Victoria from Windsor. 'How I dread the week after next – & how I wish it was months and years off! The nearer the fatal day approaches, the more my invincible dislike to Auntie's marriage (NOT to dear Liko) – increases. Sometimes I feel as if I *never* cld take her myself to the Marriage Service – & that I wld wish to run away & hide myself!'

No doubt to the annoyance of the Hohenzollerns, the dignity of 'Royal Highness' was conferred on Prince Henry, and the exclusive Order of the Garter was bestowed at a private investiture. In spite of the sharp exchange of notes between the Queen and the Prussian royal house, she allowed Liko to wear the exquisite white uniform of the *Gardes du Corps*, with glistening breastplate and eagle-mounted helmet – an impressive sight which provoked the Prince of Wales to quip: 'Here comes Beatrice's Lohengrin!' The remark of a gossip-columnist contained more sting. Commenting upon the alacrity with which Prince Henry had answered 'Yes' while making the marriage vow, he observed: 'It is not vouchsafed to all of us to decome demorganaticated, bridegrooms, Royal Highnesses, and Knights of the Garter in the twinkling of an eye.'

Whatever the cynics might say, this marriage was visible proof to the Battenbergs that they had passed directly into the circle of Queen Victoria's children.

The matriarch's earlier fears were groundless, as she noted in her *Journal* on the wedding night. In her belief, a happier-looking couple 'could seldom be seen kneeling at the altar together. It was very touching. I stood very close to my dear child, who looked very sweet, pure and calm. Though I stood for the ninth time near a child and for the fifth time near a daughter at the altar, I never felt more deeply than I did on this occasion, though full of confidence.'

Since her own marriage, the Queen had leaned heavily on others: first the consort, then Disraeli, Brown and Beatrice. Now there was a sturdy Battenberg. Prince Henry quickly appreciated how exacting this would be. The honeymoon was restricted to a mere two days before Beatrice and Liko were reunited with the Queen. The Duke of Cambridge wrote in his diary: 'At 5, we saw the young couple drive off for their honeymoon to Lady Cochrane's Villa near Ryde ... We all dined in uniform in the two large tents. The Queen was again present and seemed wonderfully cheerful and well. The Gardens were beautifully illuminated and the *Hector* and Royal Yacht, besides being illuminated, gave a very pretty display of fireworks.'

Some days later Prince Henry took the oath of allegiance at the House of Lords, but it was discovered that, in the flurry, he had not been naturalized. Thus a bill was quickly passed in Parliament. Naturalization did not, however, win him easy popularity. In his mixed ancestral background, Liko was part German and part Polish, and although he would eventually win the people's respect, at first his background did not endear itself. These initial stages, indeed, must have been exacting. His wife was much more developed intellectually – and far more mature and rigid in her mode of life. The hallmark of the Battenbergs stamped them essentially as men of action, yet Liko lacked even a home of his own and had to assume a more passive role. One visualizes the ex-Prussian guardee not merely pandering to the matriarch's whims but aimlessly admiring Beatrice's aviary of canaries and doves.

Gradually, however, even some of the Queen's more obdurate ways receded before Battenberg charm. The measure of Liko's gradual influence can be gauged by Victoria's gradual relaxation of her strictures against tobacco. The Queen, who could tell by smelling a letter whether the writer had been smoking, had banned the use of tobacco in the royal homes, but now Liko persuaded her to devote one room to smokers at Osborne. At Windsor Castle, however, the practice was still rigidly confined to the billiards room after eleven at night.

To the man whom the Queen would describe as the 'sunbeam in our home', she began to reveal the contents of state papers. This was a confidence which the matriarch wrongly refused to accord even to the heir to the throne. It is likely that the trust which the Queen foolishly denied the Prince of Wales, yet placed unhesitatingly in the Battenbergs, rankled with him. Probably latent irritation accounted for his outburst in January 1892, on the death of Prince Albert Victor, his eldest son. Desiring to make the funeral ceremony at Windsor extremely private, the Princess of Wales requested that all ladies should be absent. A stickler for tradition, the Queen overruled the request. Due to the spread of influenza, the doctors advised Victoria to stay away, but she permitted her daughters to attend. When the ceremony was over – to their annoyance – the door of their pew could not be opened for some time. When the matter was duly reported, Sir Henry Ponsonby, raising the matter with one of the Prince's equerries, was informed:

... The Prince of Wales desires me to say that – the harem of Princesses was *not* locked into the further Zenana pew closet but the door got jammed, and adds that they were none of them wanted at all. No ladies were to attend, and the Princess of Wales especially requested privacy – and to avoid meeting her Osborne relations. So they all came.

If Princess Beatrice was annoyed, it cannot be helped and she must get over it – as she likes!

The influence of Prince Henry of Battenberg over the Queen was testified by his sister Marie, after a visit to Windsor in 1886. She revealed that since Liko had joined the Queen's household, many of her

peculiar habits have disappeared. She wears robes of lighter colour, and she enjoys the company of guests and music. I have never felt more German than when with her, who is so proud of her German descent, and who knew how to foster the sense of kinship. The Queen has many German ways, for example she likes to soak her cake in her coffee, which in England is absolutely forbidden. She speaks a quite classic German, without the slightest foreign accent ...

The most interesting time is at breakfast: the Queen then generally discussed with us the latest political events suggested by ministerial despatches, which are brought to her in steel boxes.

The presence of the Battenbergs in the royal homes renewed the Queen with vitality, and Victoria's long period of seclusion came to an end. Republicanism, which had tried to root itself in that melancholy climate, now withered before the wild public acclaim as the Queen paraded in public. Until then the republican movement had begun to thrive among middle-class radicals and the working-class. The Chartists had confidently, yet inaccurately, assumed that when the workers secured political power the monarchy would disappear with the House of Lords and other relics of the Middle Ages. In the 1860s republican sentiment had hardened, purely because of the Queen's perversity. Her promptness to accumulate a fortune out of the Civil List without fulfilling her public functions was resented.

But now the little black figure, driving in the coach, won back the people's affection. Prince Henry and Princess Beatrice were seen increasingly with her. Liko draped the Queen's wraps but never assumed the prerogatives of her sons. Yet the Battenbergs – certainly Princess Beatrice – were more respected than the Prince of Wales by many of the people. It is unlikely that many of the citizens shared the extreme view of Charles Bradlaugh, a Member of Parliament, who wrote that it was his 'earnest desire that the present Prince of Wales should never dishonour this country by becoming king', but, involved in a baccarat scandal and the divorce court, the behaviour of the Prince, who was nicknamed 'Guelpho the Gay', was questioned by some of the populace.

Even if he resented the manner with which Liko had ingratiated himself into the Queen's goodwill, the Prince of Wales did not appear to bear malice towards his brother-in-law. Indeed, it is said that the heir to the throne preferred the companionship of Prince Henry to that of some of his own brothers. Liko appealed because of his informality – an attribute which would be manifest in Prince Philip, Duke of Edinburgh, years later.

6

War and Revolution

Like the Prince of Wales, Prince Henry did not lack his critics, who accused him of indolence. The barbs of the *Punch* cartoonists probably pierced deeply. They insinuated that his primary contribution to the nation – in return for his annuity from the Civil List – was playing billiards with the Queen's Private Secretary.

To taunt royalty had been a cartoonist's prerogative over the years, and it was often perfectly justified. But to cavil as regards Prince Henry of Battenberg was ill-placed and frivolous. Yet when Parliament, on Gladstone's motion, had voted Princess Beatrice a dowry of £30,000 and an annuity of £6,000 – passed by 337 votes to 38 – a large cartoon showed Princess Beatrice, in the guise of a cook, rolling pastry on the kitchen table. The flour bin bore the figure of £30,000, and seated on a wooden chair Prince Henry was shown peeling potatoes. 'Well, Harry, dear, this is Holy Matrimoney,' ran the caption, and Prince Henry replied: 'No, Trixie, darling, not *wholly* a matter of money.' The cartoonists also grasped at the forthcoming birth of the Battenbergs' first child to make snide observations, emphasizing that Liko had been aggrandized by marrying the Queen's daughter.

Such comment was baseless and underestimated the importance of Prince Henry's services. Though on a far lesser scale, he was wearing the mantle of the late Prince Consort and as a close companion and aide during the Queen's travels abroad, Liko's assistance was of immense value.

A son, christened Alexander Albert after his grandfathers, was born to the Battenbergs at Windsor at five o'clock on the morning of 23 November 1886. At that time the Grandmama of Europe had thirty-six grandchildren and a number of great-grandchildren, but 'Drino's' arrival was unique in that it marked a new phase in the Queen's declining years. The happiness which Prince Henry's companionship had brought was intensified, and increased with the birth of three more Battenberg children.

Princess Beatrice gave birth to a daughter, the first royal baby to be born in Scotland since 1600, at Balmoral on 24 October 1887. The christening on 23 November at St Giles's Cathedral, Edinburgh, was equally distinctive. The exiled French Empress Eugénie, then living in a rambling old mansion at Farnborough Hill, was one of the infant's sponsors. The child's names should have been Victoria Eugénie Julia Eua –

Princess Beatrice taking the last name from Gallic mythology – but Sir Cameron Lees, officiating at the ceremony, misread the 'u' for 'n', and the baby destined to marry into the Bourbon family was henceforth known as 'Ena'.

The Battenbergs' third child, Leopold, tragically a haemophiliac, was born on 21 May 1889, at Windsor, three days before the matriarch's seventieth birthday. Misfortune attended the boy from the start; a dislocated hip would eventually deteriorate into chronic lameness. Indeed, his life would bear comparison with the fate of that other Prince Leopold, his maternal uncle. The birth of a third son – destined to die in battle – at Balmoral on 3 October 1891, again sparked off jubilation in Scotland. To commemorate his birthplace, the name Donald was included with Maurice Victor. The gold font travelled northwards for the christening, and the baby Prince was baptized in the castle drawing-room, witnessed by the artist, Sir George Reid, who recorded the ceremony on canvas.

At Windsor in her declining years, the children of Victoria's favourite daughter ensured hours of unassailable happiness for the aged Queen. The little Leopold 'was so like in his ways and looks to my dear Leopold' (who had died at the age of thirty), and the golden-haired Ena revived memories of her darling Benjamina's own child-hood. Sadly, the Battenberg children, who called the Queen 'Gangan', would grow up deprived of paternal guidance.

Marriage had doubtless elevated Liko; he now lived within the ambience of Europe's foremost seat of power. But the price was imposing its strain. The Queen had made him a Privy Councillor, Governor and Captain on the Isle of Wight, Governor of Carisbrooke Castle, and Honorary Colonel of the Isle of Wight Rifles. She had presented him with a yacht in which to cruise, and there was scope to indulge his love of sport and theatricals. But Battenbergs, by both temperament and tradition, were essentially men of action. A sinecure was no substitute for excitement. Prince Henry envied his brother Louis, then captain of the *Cambrian*, a cruiser of 15,000 tons, who was cutting a niche for himself in the navy. And despite the hazards in Bulgaria, both Sandro and Francis Joseph had experienced the acrid smell of gunfire in battle. Liko chafed under his inactivity, circumscribed by the irksome rules formulated years earlier by the long-dead Prince Albert. Probably what bored him most of all were the Queen's own tiresome demands, disliking him to be absent from the royal household for anything but short periods. He travelled, for instance, to Albania, to shoot, but the matriarch condemned it as a very foolish venture – 'and I hope he won't be very long away and come back safe'.

Gilded though it might be, Liko yearned to break free from the stultifying effects of the royal cage.

During March 1895, while the Queen and Princess Beatrice spent a spring holiday in France, Louis embarked alone in his yacht on what developed into an extended voyage. The press misinterpreted the trip, but the rumours were dispelled when Liko and Beatrice travelled to Kronberg in August to see Friedrichshof, a new residence

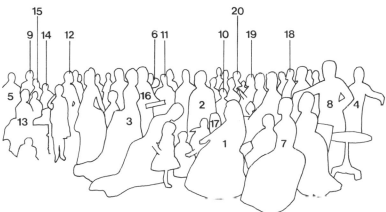

This painting by Laurence Tuxen shows Queen Victoria at Windsor in 1887. Her large European family connections also reflected the various Battenberg associations. 1 Queen Victoria. 2 The future Edward VII. 3 Princess of Wales. 4 Prince Albert Victor. 5 The future George V. 6 Prince Maud of Wales. 7 German Crown Princess. 8 German Crown Prince. 9 The future Kaiser William II. 10 Princess Sophie of Germany (later Queen Sophie of the Hellenes). 11 Princess Alicky of Hesse (eventually Tsarina of Russia). 12 Duke of Edinburgh. 13 Duchess of Edinburgh. 14 Princess Marie of Edinburgh. 15 Princess Victoria Melita of Edinburgh. 16 Duke of Connaught. 17 Princess Margaret of Connaught. 18 Prince Louis of Battenberg. 19 Princess Beatrice holding Princess Ena (future Queen of Spain). 20 Prince Henry of Battenberg.

which the Empress Frederick had erected in the Taunus forest. But never again would the Battenbergs spend a holiday together.

Contrary to a treaty of 1874, King Prempeh of Ashanti had unleashed an orgy of human sacrifice and slave trading, choosing his victims from the neighbouring Gold Coast. The British Government decided to send out a punitive force and, rather surprisingly, the Queen consented to allow Prince Christian, the eldest son of her daughter Helena, to accompany it. Prince Henry of Battenberg, keen to escape from the rather stifling atmosphere of the Court, seized his chance. Some days later, while taking breakfast, he requested the startled Queen to grant him permission as well. 'I told him it would never do,' wrote Victoria, but Liko, with his wife's support, was firm. The Queen relented and actually agreed that it was a very gallant thing to do. The concession, however, came neither easily nor quickly. The matriarch summoned her physician, Sir James Reid, who outlined the inherent dangers, especially the risk of disease which had already exacted a frightful toll of British lives. Liko countered that he was anxious to prove his devotion to his adopted country.

Cynics connected with certain newpapers, and in various clubs, interpreted his gesture erroneously. Typical was the false insinuation that Liko would not accompany his battalion but sail in luxury on a liner leaving Liverpool. Prince Henry, however, assured Lord Harris that he was an Englishman, 'and I want to show the people of England that I am ready to take the rough with the smooth. I know there is no glory and honour to be got out of it, and I know of the danger of subsequent ill-health and perhaps death from malaria, which I know is so great in that country.' The reality underlying these words would be etched incisively on the national mind, confounding contemptible rumour.

When, on 6 December, Colonel Prince Henry of Battenberg knelt and kissed the Queen's hand in farewell, the matriarch believed that every precaution had been taken to guarantee her son-in-law's safety; his safe return by February, if not before, seemed certain. The bands played *Auld Lang Syne* as the troop train steamed slowly out of Aldershot the following day. The scene had latent poignancy: Liko's final wave would be Beatrice's last glimpse of her husband alive. When he returned, he would be dead, his body preserved against equatorial heat in a tank improvised from biscuit tins and filled with rum.

Two days after their arrival, on Christmas Day, at Cape Coast Castle, the British force began the exhausting march to Kumasi. In sweltering heat, the journey took the men through bush, forest and swamp, a malarial death-trap that had already taken casualties when the Pra river was sighted a week later. The speed with which the fever struck was most alarming. Strolling one evening with Major Ferguson, the camp commandant, at Prahsu, Liko noted that his companion bore the first signs of the fever. Two days later the officer was dead.

With this unnerving threat to life, and as 'the climate was beginning to tell on the troops', the column carried on to Kwisa. Here Liko, showing the first symptoms of

Princess Beatrice with her son,
Prince Maurice of Battenberg. His
death in the First World War
coincided with his uncle's dismissal
from the Admiralty.

Prince Henry and Princess
Beatrice's other children: (left to
right) Leopold, Victoria Eugénie
(the future Queen of Spain) and
Alexander who received the title of
Marquess of Carisbrooke.

The British royal family at Osborne. (Left to right) Prince Leopold of Battenberg,
Princess Aribert of Anhalt, the future Edward VIII, the Princess of Wales, Princess Mary,
Princess Margaret of Connaught, Prince Alexander of Battenberg, the future George VI,
the Prince of Wales (later George V), Queen Victoria, Prince Arthur of Connaught, the
Duchess of Connaught, Princess Patricia of Connaught, Princess Beatrice, Princess Ena of
Battenberg, Princess Victoria of Schleswig-Holstein and Prince Maurice of Battenberg.

malaria, was ordered back to base, borne by natives on a stretcher. He reached Cape Coast Castle on 17 January. The fever had grown decidedly worse but, when he was carried aboard the *Blonde*, there was still no cause for anxiety as the ship steamed for England. Yet Liko never saw his adopted country again; he died on 20 January, the day when King Prempeh surrendered at Kumasi. 'In case I die, tell the Princess from me that I came here not to win glory but from a sense of duty,' were his last words for his wife. Thinking that her husband was recovering, Beatrice had planned to join Liko during his convalescence in Madeira. She had received an earlier telegram to that effect, only to be informed now that he was dead. 'The life is gone out of me,' she said in her grief. 'God in his mercy help us!' wrote the Queen, 'It seems as if the years '61 and '62 had returned ...' Mother and daughter had entered widowhood at the identical age of thirty-eight.

Transferred from the *Blonde* to the *Blenheim*, the body of Prince Henry reached Portsmouth on the morning of 4 February. The coffin lay in the captain's cabin, where Princess Beatrice, the Prince of Wales, the Duke of Connaught, Princess Christian, the Princes Louis and Francis Joseph of Battenberg, and the Grand Duke Ernest of Hesse, assembled for a service conducted by the Bishop of Winchester and a naval chaplain. 'The sunbeam in our Home is *gone*!' wrote the Queen to her granddaughter Vicky. 'It breaks my heart to think of darling Auntie & her darling Children. Ludwig [Louis] was so kind & affte to her & to poor dear little Drino – & Franzjos [Francis Joseph] too – their grief was so affecting ... I can hardly bear associating ... with those who were not with me at that terrible time, & to hear Georgie's little boy call him "Papa" & to think of our poor little darlings who can no longer do so, was terribly upsetting.'

As he had earlier requested, Prince Henry was buried at Whippingham Church. Behind the coffin walked Butcher, his servant in Africa, who was present at his death; a groom leading Liko's favourite hunter; and the captain of his yacht, *Sheilah*. In due course, a monument marked his grave: a sarcophagus bearing a recumbent figure and adorned with columns of green and white marble from Iona, an island which Prince Henry had loved.

In the little memorial chapel at Heiligenberg, there are bronze reliefs in memory of Liko and Sandro: Alexander of Bulgaria resting with the emblems of war in his coffin, and Henry sleeping in a skiff guided homeward by angels.

In the last five years of Queen Victoria's life, Prince Henry's offspring were her favourite grandchildren. The care and affection that she bestowed on them must have been substantial, for when Drino first went to Wellington College, he confessed that the wrench from the Queen was greater than from his mother. He set out on a naval career, joining the *Britannia* on leaving school, but transferred to the army in 1908. In May 1917, while he was fighting with the Grenadier Guards in France during the First World War, it was announced that the name Battenberg had been anglicized to 'Mountbatten'. As the Marquess of Carisbrooke, Earl of Berkhamsted and Viscount Launceston, he became a member of the peerage on 17 July, and within two days celebrated his marriage to Lady Irene Denison, the only daughter of the second Earl of Londesborough.

Most likely Drino would have progressed to military eminence, but he abandoned the Battenberg tradition and entered commerce – the first member of the royal family, incidentally, to do so. The first signs of his business acumen had been detected at school. When he had asked the Queen to resolve a money problem, she declined, sternly admonishing him to keep within his allowance. Soon he informed his grandmother that he was no longer in financial straits, having sold her recent letter. Devoid of any knowledge of the business world, Drino was thirty-three when he was accepted as a junior clerk in the City bank of Lazard Brothers and later his name appeared on the boards of certain prominent companies.

At the outset of the Second World War, volunteering for duties with the Royal Air Force, he served as a non-flying officer against the country of his father's origin. He died in 1959, three years after his wife. Lady Iris Mountbatten, who worked for a while in a New York store, is their sole child.

The other sons of Prince Henry of Battenberg never achieved old age. But for his unstable health and disability, Leopold would have wholeheartedly welcomed a military career. Instead, inheriting the intellectual attributes of Princess Beatrice, his was a scholar's life after studying at Magdalene College, Cambridge. Always a bachelor, and sharing his mother's apartments at Kensington Palace, Leopold travelled extensively. The First World War enabled him to experience the militarism for which he hankered. In normal circumstances, his lameness debarred him from donning uniform, yet King George v and Lord Kitchener yielded to his persistence to enlist on the outbreak of hostilities. Ignoring his inflamed hip and chronic sciatica, when the Isle of Wight Rifles crossed the English Channel to France, Leopold went with them. He was mentioned in despatches and attained the rank of major as a member of an advanced divisional staff.

His adverse health worsened dramatically after the war, but he found in his mother a devoted nurse. It was all the more tragic, therefore, that, while Beatrice was taking a short respite in Sicily, her son died on 22 April 1922. An emergency operation at Kensington Palace had been imperative. Only nurses and staff were at his bedside when he died. He was only thirty-three.

His younger brother Maurice held a commission in the 60th (King's Royal) Rifles after leaving Sandhurst. The death in the Boer War of his cousin Prince Christian Victor, who had accompanied Prince Henry to Ashanti, had not deterred him in boyhood. Christian had lost his life while also serving with the 60th Rifles, and his sister, Princess Helena Victoria, was staying at Balmoral with the Queen and Princess Beatrice when she learned of her brother's death. In his dressing-gown that evening Maurice went to the room of the distressed Princess and said: 'Cousin Thora, it may comfort you to know that I have decided to join the 60th when I am old enough.'

Maurice was essentially of the Battenberg mould: a lover of sports and invention. He enthused over the new and exciting means of transport – aviation – learning to fly the then primitive aircraft. Making solo flights from Hendon, he had ambitions to transfer to the newly-formed Royal Flying Corps, but it was an aspiration that was never fulfilled. As the Germans began to overrun Europe, Maurice accompanied his regiment to France, plunging into front-line action at the outset.

Indeed, the holocaust was merely two months old when Maurice was mentioned in despatches. An eye-witness related that, after the retreat from Mons, 'an order came to our company that a bridge must be taken at once. It was blocked with carts, broken furniture, glass and barbed wire. Lieutenant Battenberg told us that we must get through. He was first man over it, during a murderous enemy bombardment, a brave act for a young officer to do alone and thus inspire his men.' Some weeks later, on 27 October, a few days after his twenty-third birthday, Prince Maurice sustained a fatal shrapnel wound. His epitaph crystallized the traits of Prince Henry of Battenberg's courageous son: 'Those who shared with Maurice of Battenberg the perils and glories, the happiness and the miseries of life at "the front", will retain memories of his pluck, his lovable nature and his good comradeship. For all he had a cheery, kindly word, and all had a kindly word for him.'

When Lord Kitchener asked if she wished to have her son's body returned to England, Princess Beatrice preferred to let him lie with his comrades at Ypres.

For Princess Beatrice, domestic duties multiplied after her husband's death. Living mostly in the tranquillity of Osborne, everything conformed to the needs of the ageing Queen. Victoria's eyesight was failing, and she was becoming increasingly dependent on Princess Beatrice. Although such duties could have been entrusted to her secretaries, the matriarch insisted that Beatrice should open her vast number of letters and read them aloud.

In this compact daily pattern, the lives of the Battenberg children were entwined with their grandmother's. In their earlier years they breakfasted with her – beneath her parasol tent on the lawns on fine days, indoors when the weather was bad. After morning studies, they visited 'Gangan' for dessert at lunchtime, then returned to her for tea. They played in her sitting-room, and a ride in grandmama's bath-chair guaranteed moments of joy. They were the warm ray that dissipated the gloom of earlier years. 'I love those darling children so,' the old Queen once declared, 'almost as much as their own parents.'

Being an only daughter, perhaps Princess Ena received that little extra affection from the matriarch. Golden-haired, blue-eyed, with a healthy complexion, Ena developed tomboyish characteristics, which was not surprising considering the influence of three

The Marquess of
Carisbrooke (left) was the
first member of the British
royal family to enter
commerce. Vice-President of
the Warrant Holders'
Association he is seen here
welcoming guests to one of
their luncheons.

Lord Leopold Mountbatten,
unable to pursue a military
career through ill-health,
accepted a scholar's life after
studying at Cambridge.

energetic brothers. A devotee of the open air, she could row, ride, and manoeuvre a fishing-rod with skill. Years later she would be expert at tennis and golf.

In the circumstances, the death of Queen Victoria wrought a decisive change for Princess Beatrice and her family. For Beatrice, gone was the palace enslavement but with it the close intimacy of Victoria's Court. Now, in its place, was her brother's glittering circle, in which the Princess, who was well known for her diffidence, felt rather ill at ease. At Court, Beatrice had been displaced – a fact which imprinted itself when Osborne House was transferred to the navy.

During 1904, not long after her seventeenth birthday, Princess Ena was invited by King Edward VII to go with her mother – who now resided at Osborne Cottage – to stay temporarily at Buckingham Palace – 'as he wished me to come out officially', Ena explained later. She had clearly inherited Prince Henry's charm and penchant for games, and from the maternal side Princess Beatrice's talents for music and drawing. Yet the dignity and flashing smile were a mere façade that concealed a profoundly sensitive nature. The Empress Frederick would observe with prophetic insight: 'Ena has a charming disposition, so affectionate and full of feeling. She is so sensitive that I fear she will never find life easy.' Her future, which was to be strewn with tragedy and drama, was determined by a visit to England of the nineteen-year-old Spanish King in June 1905.

Alfonso XIII was a sovereign even in his mother's womb, for his father, the courteous Alfonso XII, had died six months before his birth. Thus, until his coming of age on his sixteenth birthday, his mother, the stiff-backed Maria Cristina – a former Arch-duchess of Austria – had served as regent. They had been uneasy years, and the thread that bound the monarchy to the people was now tenuous. It was therefore the fervent desire of Alfonso's ministers that he should marry and secure the succession, for the anarchists and their bombs were not confined to Holy Russia; neither was assassination something new. The strife and revolution of nineteenth-century Spain had spilled over into modern times as Alfonso's inheritance.

Spain had been infected with republicanism for many years. Moreover, the debonair but tubercular Alfonso XII was not a popular king, and dissatisfaction with the Bourbons was therefore rife at the time of his death at the age of twenty-nine, imposing a formidable task on his widow, Maria Cristina of Austria, and a precarious inheritance for his son, Alfonso XIII. A hazardous tenure thus awaited anyone who consented to be the young King's bride.

Germany had a surfeit of marriageable princesses. The Kaiser William II, anxious to arrange a dynastic alliance with the Bourbons, arrived at Vigo with typical bombast ostensibly to review the Spanish fleet. His uncle, King Edward VII, displayed less impatience and greater aplomb, deputing his brother the Duke of Connaught, to confer the Order of the Garter on the young Alfonso. In this subtle way the King focused on Patricia, the Duke's daughter, whom he ranked as the ideal bride. Liberal politicians in Spain also favoured a link with the British Court.

In Paris on his journey to London, Alfonso came near to death; a Spanish anarchist threw a 'pineapple' bomb beneath the young King's carriage. Whatever Alfonso's shortcomings, he did not lack courage and reached Buckingham Palace unperturbed the next day.

During a week of banquets and dazzling ceremonial, Alfonso discovered that the Princess Patricia resisted his Bourbon charm. During a supper party, the chair on the King's right remained significantly vacant, Patricia preferring the companionship of a guardsman on the balcony. At a luncheon given by the Duke of Connaught the following day, Alfonso could contain himself no longer. Turning to the Duchess of Westminster on his left, he asked: 'Am I very ugly? ... I do not please the lady [Princess Patricia] on my right.'

The King, however, was not dismayed. Asked if any of the young ladies had attracted him, he replied: 'The fair one', referring to Princess Ena, whom he had first seen on the night of his arrival.

The betrothal was vehemently opposed in Anglican quarters when the news leaked out that following March. In the uproar, letters to *The Times* fiercely stressed that the Royal Marriage Act strictly forbade marriages with Catholics. 'Beatrice', wrote the Prince of Wales (the future King George V) to his wife, 'is advised ... to keep Ena quiet somewhere at Osborne and not to bring her to London as the feeling is very strong.'

Reactionaries in Spain were just as vociferous in condemning the match, and certain European royalties raised the bogey of the morganatic Battenbergs yet again. The Grand Duchess of Mecklenburg-Strelitz wrote to Princess May, her niece: 'So Ena is to become Spanish Queen! A Battenberg, good gracious!' Not surprisingly the Kaiser William, never missing the chance to malign Princess Julie of Battenberg's descendants, stupidly showered contempt on the proposed union. But Edward VII was unmoved. Allowing neither the faith nor carping criticism to obstruct, he announced that 'Princess Victoria Eugénie of Battenberg will sign a document formally renouncing her and her descendants' rights to the English throne on becoming a Roman Catholic.'

On 7 March 1906, while visiting Queen Maria Cristina at San Sebastian, Ena was received into the Catholic Church. The wedding was planned for 31 May of that year – the anniversary of the attempt to assassinate the King in France.

With their retinues, royal personalities in Europe gravitated to Paris to board the *Sud Express* for Madrid; despite the social élite that it carried the train was said to be undeniably dirty. Chaos awaited them at the Spanish frontier town of Irun until everyone was at last installed in coaches that, due to the colossal heat, felt like ovens.

About three the next afternoon, the royalties, dusty and dishevelled, set foot in Madrid for a wedding ceremony that contained the essence of medieval splendour darkened by death. On that memorable wedding-day, a tremor of anxiety beset the guests as their coaches lumbered through the noisy streets to the Church of San Jeronimo. The shrine itself presented an even greater hazard. As Princess Ena's aunt,

Princess Marie of Battenberg, revealed later: 'During the ceremony the thought suddenly occurred to me how easy it would be in the narrow, one-aisled church for an attempt to be made from above on all this princely assemblage. I little knew, then, by what a hair's breadth we had escaped the danger.'

The large-scale slaughter of European royalties was avoided by the flimsiest chance. Previously indisposed, an American journalist now felt well enough to attend the wedding, claiming the ticket of admission which would otherwise have been received by an assassin, the son of a Barcelona tradesman, posing as a newsman. Thus frustrated, Matteo Morral, a disciple of a well-known anarchist, went to a four-storey-high balcony overlooking the Calle Mayor, the old narrow high street of Madrid. Morral had a bouquet that concealed a bomb, but luckily, as the procession wound its way to the palace from the church, the royal coach stopped, and Morral hurled his flowers some seconds too soon. Suddenly there was a lurid flame, a nauseating smell, the screaming of wounded horses.

Our carriage [later explained the Prince of Wales] was just in front of the one which Queen Cristina and Aunt Beatrice were driving, and they were just ahead of Alfonso and Ena who were at the end of the procession. Just before our carriage reached the Palace, we heard a loud report and thought it was the first gun of a salute. We soon learned however that when about 200 yards from the Palace in a narrow street, the Calle Mayor, close to the Italian Embassy, a bomb was thrown ... at the King and Queen's carriage. It burst between the wheel horses and the front of the carriage, killing about 20 people and wounding about 50 or 60, mostly officers and soldiers. Thank God! Alfonso and Ena were not touched although covered with glass from the broken windows. The Marquesa Torlosa and her niece were killed. They were standing on a balcony just below the window from which the bomb was thrown. The two wheelers were killed and another horse, the carriage however went about 30 yards. Sir M. de Bunsen (the British ambassador), Morgan, Lowther (the military attaché) and the four officers of the 16th Lancers were in a house close by, rushed out ... and assisted Ena out of the carriage, both she and Alfonso showed great courage and presence of mind. They got into another carriage at once and drove off to the Palace amid frantic cheering.

... they let him [the anarchist] escape. I believe the Spanish police and detectives are about the worst in the world. No precautions whatever had been taken, they are the most happy go lucky people here ... Eventually we had lunch about 3. I proposed their healths, not easy after the emotions caused by this terrible affair.

The excitement at the palace was indescribable, wrote Ena's Aunt Marie, yet 'Ena was incredibly self-controlled, in spite of the deadly shock ... but she kept on repeating: "I saw a man without any legs."' Tactlessly in that tense atmosphere, the Russian-born Duchess of Edinburgh loudly told those around her: 'I am so accustomed to that sort of thing.' She was, however, merely telling the truth: after determined attempts anarchists had sadistically deprived her father, Nicholas II, and her brother, the Grand Duke Serge, of their lives.

82

The bomb attack on King
Alfonso and Queen Ena in
the Calle Mayor, Madrid,
after their wedding in May
1906. Ena's 'long Calvary'
lay ahead.

King Alfonso XIII of Spain
and Queen Ena. Because of
the unstable political
situation, the couple's reign
was never easy.

Morral was arrested in a village near Escorial some days later, but on his way to prison he first shot his guard and then turned the gun on himself.

Violent death seemed to be an intrinsic facet of life in that torrid heat. At the behest of Parliament, the British representatives were excused from attending the festival bull-fight. The new Queen shared the revulsion of her kinfolk, blotting out the brutal scenes by wearing opaque glasses that marred her vision. 'I felt horrified,' wrote Aunt Marie, 'but stood it out, for Ena had not only to control herself, but to smile ... "Once in my life, and never again," I thought. Poor Ena will have to go through it over and over again.'

Morral's lethal bouquet was an ill omen. Ahead of the eighteen-year-old Queen Ena lay her 'long Calvary'. From the safety of Britain this unsophisticated girl was now the mistress of the most formal yet flamboyant Court in Europe. Royal etiquette had barely changed since the sixteenth century. Pomp and protocol, allied with the burning fervour of Spanish Catholicism, invested life with a sense of endless pageantry. The Cross and the Crown were inseparable.

The Prince and Princess of Wales had been intrigued by the elaborate detail and consistency of Court ritual whenever they left their apartments at the Palacio Real – always, incidentally, attended by a duke. A colourfully uniformed halberdier, springing to attention at the clap of an official's hands, briskly presented arms, shouting '*Arriba Princesa! Arriba Principe!*' – a cry which would be repeated successively as the royal couple progressed along the ornate corridors. As a novelty it could be fascinating – even amusing – but as an essential part of life it imposed a strain.

On the domestic scene loomed the pious, unpretentious yet dominant figure of Queen Maria Cristina, Ena's mother-in-law. The marriage of Princess Ena to her son had in a sense begun Maria Cristina's crucifixion, for the secret of the Battenbergs – as it was occasionally called – was known to her. She was aware that Ena's brother, Leopold, was definitely affected by the 'royal disease' and feared that marriage might taint Bourbon blood. Maria Cristina's forebodings were not solely out of concern for the possible miseries of a future offspring, but also for the safety of Bourbon rule in Spain. No one could be certain, of course, that Ena was herself a carrier; she was radiant with good health and possessed great vitality. From the beginning King Alfonso had been warned but, as was apparent when he was at the wheel of a car, by nature he was ready to accept risks.

In May 1907, Queen Ena gave birth to a son. Jubilantly King Alfonso carried the child on a golden, lace-covered tray to the throne-room, proudly exhibiting his heir to the assembled élite. The Pope agreed to be one of the godfathers and bestowed the Order of the Golden Rose on the Queen. Spain rejoiced by celebrating with fiestas for a week. Tragically, however, it was the beginning of parental grief. Alfonso, Prince of the Asturias, was such an acute haemophiliac that when the parents eventually fled from Spain, he had to leave Madrid on a stretcher.

A second son, Don Jaime, Duke of Segovia, was born deaf and dumb. Another child was stillborn. Fortunately two daughters – the Infantas Beatriz and Maria Cristina – were healthy, as was the third son, Don Juan, Count of Barcelona. The fourth son, Don Gonzalo, was yet another victim of the dread affliction. This congenital ailment inspired many people of influence, especially among the reactionaries and in the Church, to speak against the 'foreign Queen'. They could not forget her former Protestantism and her penchant for dancing, tennis and golf – pleasures which they considered were not in keeping with the dignity of the Queen of Spain.

The news of the wretched family's sufferings had its repercussions in Britain, too. Apparently, some members of the royal family felt that Princess Ena had been sacrificed to a Bourbon degenerate, that the Bourbons were haemophiliacs to a man and that the Princess had been forced to embrace the Catholic religion against her will. They were particularly horrified by the suggestion that Ena had acted as a tire-woman to the corpse of the Queen Mother, in keeping with Spanish tradition.

Queen Ena experienced profound unhappiness over her children. The unvarnished truth, however, must be that – like her cousin, the Tsarina Alicky – her mental sufferings sprang mainly from the inexorable knowledge that she was the innocent executioner of her sons.

Like their counterparts in Russia, the King and Queen of Spain were key figures in the rich pageantry of the Church. They participated, for instance, in elaborate masses and at the Lavatorio ritual on Maundy Thursday – one of the Holy Week ceremonies – when the King washed the feet of twelve aged people at the Royal Palace in Madrid. Then on Good Friday he would pardon three murderers said to be awaiting execution; as each chained man was led into the chapel where the King knelt, Alfonso forgave him – 'as I hope by the grace of God one day to be forgiven. Go in peace.' If the King saw a priest in the streets bearing the Host to the sick, it was imperative to dismount and offer the cleric his coach, then proceed himself on foot. That was why the *coche de respeto*, 'coach of respect', preceded the royal carriage on state processions; that had been the coach to which Ena and Alfonso had transferred after Morral hurled his bomb.

Queen Ena was also involved in this pious ritual. The problems, indeed, that confronted them were common to both. Apart from the common factor of haemophilia, each lived in an atmosphere steeped in religion and superstition. Revolution was a constant threat. Each knew that if news of the haemophiliac taint was ever leaked to the people, it was doubtful if the dynasty would survive.

A major difference between Ena and Alicky, however, was that the latter was comforted by a devoted and kindly spouse; Ena, unfortunately, was not. The mercurial Alfonso XIII was not without good qualities, but constancy and tenderness were not among them. The Queen predicted her own fate. 'He tires of everything,' she once remarked, referring to the restless King, 'some day he will tire of me.' As the years passed, the sufferings of their children widened the marital rift. The haemophiliac condition of the Prince of the Asturias would have even cataclysmic impact, contributing to the revolution in 1931; as the truth of his condition seeped out, it was widely interpreted that the scourge was ending the divine mandate of the House of Bourbon.

Don Gonzalo, then twenty, was the first of the royal children to die. In 1934, while motoring with his sister Beatriz in Austria, he was involved in the slightest of accidents, yet the Prince bled to death in Alfonso's arms before a priest could administer the final rites. Renouncing his claim to the throne, the Prince of the Asturias in vain tried to wrest some happiness from life. He took two Cuban wives within a relatively short period, but, like Gonzalo, an insignificant motoring accident in Miami also snatched away his life. Estranged at that time from Alfonso, the Prince was being driven along the Biscayne Boulevard when the vehicle struck a telephone pole at no great speed. He died from bleeding twelve hours later.

Rather than binding him more closely to his family, the chronic, incurable illness drove Alfonso further away. He had, however, applied every precaution to protect his haemophiliac sons; even the trees in the royal parks, it is said, had been padded.

In 1923 Elinor Glyn, the novelist, was the guest of the royal couple in Spain. She described Queen Ena as 'a fairy queen, so young and fresh and lovely', yet in those 1920s Alfonso was rumoured to be looking for other female companionship. Such behaviour did not stabilize the throne. Attempts were made on his life, and other plots were exposed. Indeed, Spain seethed with discontent. However, distinct from her cousins, Queen Marie of Roumania and the Tsarina Alicky of Russia, Queen Ena maintained a natural role in the unstable politics of the country. One can only speculate on her reaction, steeped as she was in British traditions, when the King broke his constitutional oath in 1923 and acquiesced to the military dictatorship of General Primo de Rivera.

Perhaps the inevitability of exile sometimes crossed Queen Ena's mind, for she once remarked to the Grand Duchess Marie of Russia, then exiled in Paris: 'And who, after all, can tell . . . In a very few years I might join you here.'

Military dictatorship was unpalatable to many Spaniards, but the death of Primo de Rivera in 1930 effected change. His successor, General Berenguer, ex-High Commissioner of Morocco, was chosen to prepare Spain for municipal elections, a decision which enabled the anti-monarchists to release a spate of propaganda in the urban areas. That was the state in Spain when, in January 1931, in response to a telephone call, Queen Ena hurried to London: her mother, Princess Beatrice, after fracturing her arm at Kensington Palace, had developed a bronchial complaint and was critically ill. During her absence 'Fuera el Rey' ('Away with the King') became a common cry, to which the nonchalant Alfonso remarked that he seemed to be out of fashion.

It was with astonishment, therefore, that on returning to Madrid at the end of February, Ena was welcomed by crowds crying: 'Viva la Reina!' Unfortunately it was a false augury of the future. Although at the April elections the Monarchists gained an all-over majority, anti-royalist victories in the cities gave the Republicans the signal for revolution. To avoid bloodshed, Alfonso decided to quit for a while, wrongly believing that the republican flames would die. He refused to abdicate; in a manifesto to the nation he renounced 'nothing of my rights because rather than my own, they are a deposit accumulated by history ...' The King had arranged to leave for France that night, to be followed by his family the next day, although the Prince of the Asturias, then confined to bed, was considered too weak to move. At the Palacio Real a little convoy of cars waited on the garden terrace. Bidding farewell to a loyal group who wished him well, Alfonso stepped into the leading car and vanished into the darkness.

Throughout the night a threatening crowd screamed '*Viva la Republica!*' outside the palace. As Ena and her family sat at the bedside of her haemophiliac son, a new noise caused them to rush to the windows. As they peered through the blinds, a lorry was driven into a palace door. Repeatedly it reversed and crashed again, to break it down. A squadron of Hussars intervened but the hysteria went unabated. To dally further was risky. Borrowing some money, and with restricted luggage, she and her children hurried from the palace by the garden entrance just after dawn. Too frail to stand, the Prince of the Asturias had to be carried on a stretcher. The plan was to drive to the Escorial and there board a train for Paris. Seeing some well-wishers in the Casa de Campo, Ena stopped her car and alighted. A witness of that poignant moment described how the Queen had held many courts 'in the palace on the horizon, received foreign sovereigns, been the brilliant central figure in many splendid and sumptuous ceremonials. At not one of them had she been more queenly, more royally self-controlled, more splendidly a woman than on this sun-drenched morning with a rock for her throne ... and the unfailing love of a few of her truest friends and servants as her only solace and support.'

The marriage of Ena and Alfonso, which had deteriorated while they lived in Spain, now virtually disintegrated in exile. The King lived in Rome, a devotee of the bridge table, and the Queen stayed for long periods in England with her Mountbatten relations. She was with her husband, however, when he died in 1941, at the Grand Hotel in the Italian capital. The Monarchists in Spain now proclaimed Ena's third son the Pretender to the Spanish throne. Don Juan, who had been anglicized to some degree, had trained as a cadet at Dartmouth, then served as a midshipman in the *Enterprise*. He married a cousin and resided in Portugal. But his future was uncertain.

After General Franco's victory in the civil war, Spain became theoretically a monarchy again. By a Succession Law, it was decreed that on Franco's death 'a person of royal blood' would follow him as head of state. But it would not be Don Juan; his candidacy did not receive the Caudillo's blessing, for Franco preferred Juan Carlos, the Count of Barcelona's son.

Queen Ena was as soignée as ever at her grandson's wedding in Athens to Princess Sophie of Greece. Six years later – in 1968 – Sophie gave birth to her third child, her first son. Ena travelled to Madrid for the christening. Thirty-seven years earlier she had fled in disarray from Spain. Sadly she had commented 'I thought I had done well.' With her husband she had ruled the country for twenty-five years. Now the dynasty had returned, but she never witnessed the crowning of her grandson. In April of the following year, she died at her home in Lausanne at the age of eighty-one. As the Crown Princess Frederick had prophesied, Ena had not found life easy.

7

Rise and Fall

MARITAL unhappiness was alien to Prince Louis and Princess Victoria of Battenberg who never allowed the scandal which clouded their wedding to eclipse their marriage. In 1885, soon after the birth of their daughter Alice (the future mother of Prince Philip, Duke of Edinburgh), Louis wrote of his wife to a friend: 'She is a regular sailor's wife, and takes an immense interest in all naval matters ... We are not blessed much with earthly goods, and have to live in a small way, though we are all the happier for it, I believe.'

Louis had been given a sinecure appointment in the royal yacht, the *Victoria and Albert*, but his urge to take an active part in the navy was too potent. On 30 August 1885, he was promoted to commander and spent the next four years on half-pay in the *Excellent* and *Vernon*, the gunnery and torpedo ships, then in the Mediterranean on board the new ironclad turret-ship *Dreadnought*. The latter appointment created the worst furore for Louis so far. An intimate of the Prince of Wales, Captain Sir Harry Stephenson, had requested that Louis be his executive officer and second-in-command. Critics quickly condemned the appointment as blatant favouritism. Indeed, John Redmond, the Irish Nationalist and champion of Home Rule, asked in the House of Commons if it was true that Prince Louis had been appointed 'over the heads of 30 or 40 officers having superior qualifications'. The First Lord of the Admiralty argued that Louis had been selected because he was 'best qualified for the post'. During a stormy outcry, another Irish Member announced that if Prince Louis was appointed, he would move that his salary should be disallowed.

A more moderate view in a service paper contended that if German princelings were to be denied promotion, 'they should not be admitted into the service, even when the promotion takes the form which is perhaps open to objection as a system of "taking care of Dowb". This is really the crux.'

Prince Louis would be wounded by the innuendoes of politicians and certain brother officers as he rose through the navy's hierarchy, but not until the critical days of the First World War would they deliver the *coup de grâce*. It would be absurd to deny that social status had so far lubricated the wheels of his promotion, for Louis was a favourite at Court with its inherent power, but it would be equally inane to ignore Prince Louis's undoubted talents. The ships that he commanded possessed the hallmark of brilliant efficiency. Typical was the coaling of the *Dreadnought* at Smyrna.

> From Saturday, 4.30 am until Monday forenoon [he wrote], I was in my clothes, having my meals almost always standing, and only lying on the deck, all dirty and greasy, for an hour's sleep at a time. It was very hard on the men, who worked incessantly, two halves relieving each other every two hours night and day and, having to work all through Sunday, they required a good deal of humouring. The heat was intense, and with a burning sun. On the third day I was so worn out that I could hardly drag myself along. We hoisted in close on 1,000 tons; that is, 11,000 bags which had to be filled, then hoisted in, emptied, and sent back for refilling. I wonder what a Lieutenant-Colonel of the British Army would say if he was expected to do that in time of peace as a matter of ordinary routine?

Prince Louis's first command, in 1889, was the *Scout*, a small torpedo cruiser. Louis so impressed his commander-in-chief, Admiral Sir Anthony Hoskins, that he was promoted to captain in December 1891. On the admiral's return to London in 1892, he arranged for Louis to join the Admiralty as Assistant Director of Naval Intelligence and head of the Mobilization Department, linked with the office of chief-of-staff to the Second Sea Lord. Louis's impact was now felt. He allied with progressive officers like Sir John Fisher and Lord Charles Beresford – nicknamed the 'Blue Water School' – who realized that future naval wars would be fought not in the traditional blockading of enemy ports but on the high seas. Ships and strategy would have to be adapted accordingly.

Louis's next sea appointment was to command the *Cambrian*, a new iron cruiser which, stationed in the Mediterranean, was – at royal request – twice guardship to Queen Victoria when she visited Villefranche in the spring of 1895 and 1896. Soon afterwards he attended the coronation in Russia of his sister-in-law and the new Tsar. Backed by her Prime Minister, Lord Salisbury, the Queen deputed Louis to effect détente with Prince Lobanoff-Rostofsky, the Russian Prime Minister, who was then showing enmity to Britain over Middle Eastern affairs.

It seemed as if Prince Louis had personally created his next command. In 1902 he had recommended to Lord Selborne, First Lord of the Admiralty, the formation of two detached cruiser squadrons of fast escort cruisers. During January 1905, Louis was appointed as rear-admiral to command the second of these, and flew his flag in the *Drake*. The adroitness with which he manoeuvred fast ships would become legendary.

The squadron's main voyage at this time was a cruise which, beginning on 1 August, aimed to engender good feeling with the United States and to strengthen the friendship between Canada, Newfoundland and the mother country. Louis caused a sensation by taking the squadron up the St Lawrence River to Quebec in fog so thick that all navigation had been halted. His flag-captain, Mark Kerr, explained that in the dense murk

> one little steamer, probably a tug, must have had a narrow shave. We suddenly heard a whistle almost under us on the starboard side. About thirty seconds later we felt the blast of

hot air from a funnel in our faces, and coming up from a spot right under us on our port side, and in spite of her nearness we never saw her. All this time the Admiral was walking up and down the bridge, showing no sign of anxiety, and never bothering us with useless questions or remarks when we were looking out from our station ninety feet above him. Truly a great exhibition of nerve and confidence.

Later, ignoring the pilot boats, the squadron – steaming in line ahead at speed during darkness in Chesapeake Bay and maintaining precise station at eighteen knots – brought up to the anchors full speed astern. The ships anchored off Annapolis in the morning. The Americans were so impressed that the following year Commander (later Admiral) William Sims was despatched to Britain to study Prince Louis's training methods for manoeuvre and gunnery. Years later the US Admiral Cameron Winslow confessed that the British squadron's visit had influenced the future of the US navy. Until then American ships had tended to function individually. Admiral Winslow admitted that 'if we had not seen the way your squadron worked, I do not suppose we would have worked as a fleet even now'.

In Annapolis, calling on Governor Warfield of Maryland – a great-uncle of the future Duchess of Windsor – Louis was captivated by the eighteenth-century executive mansion and Warfield hospitality. When Emma, the Governor's six-year-old daughter was introduced to him, Louis told her: 'I have a little boy just your age,' and Emma asked: 'What's his name?' He told her: 'He has nine names, one of which is Louis, but we call him Dickie.'

Prominent in Louis's itinerary were several days of entertainment in Washington, where he met President Theodore Roosevelt. 'All of those who have seen Prince Louis of Battenberg are delighted with him,' commented the *Washington Post*. 'His manner, so unassuming, and he appears so democratic, that no one felt that reserve with which Americans usually regard royalty. He is not the kind of man to whom salaams are agreeable ... every action denotes virility ... the Prince is a believer in the "simple life". He is ... attached to his home and family.'

Louis's visit stimulated a cordiality between the two fleets which would be a great advantage in the First World War. Unlike Prince Louis, Admiral Jack Fisher, who was later promoted to First Sea Lord, had at one period treated America as a potential threat, commenting: 'The late Lord Herschell who was out here ... was, I am sure, of the opinion the Yankees are dead against us. Only one quarter of the population of the United States are what you may call natives; the rest are Germans, Irish, Poles, and the scum of the earth ...' Louis even received from Fisher a memorandum in which the latter visualized war with German-American and Russian-American alliances. But after his son took an American bride, Fisher, characteristically, became a rabid pro-American.

On returning to England in February 1907, Prince Louis was appointed second-in-command of the Mediterranean station and promoted to vice-admiral. In the same year he was made commander-in-chief of the Atlantic Fleet, and by 1911 he was flying his flag with the third and fourth division of the Home Fleet. The period coincided with the desperate race to keep ahead of Germany's growing threat of dreadnoughts and battle cruisers. *Der Tag* was boastfully toasted in the Kaiser's navy.

That year – the summer of the coronation of George v and Queen Mary – Prince Louis and his wife entertained some of their Prussian relatives at Admiralty House, their home in Sheerness. Fisher is on record as having told Prince Louis that he could never expect a place on the Board of Admiralty because of his German connections, yet he had the wisdom to realize that Louis, being 'an intimate personal friend of the German Emperor's brother', and even on familiar terms with the Kaiser himself, was placed in a unique position to garner intelligence.

When the Kaiser anchored his yacht off Spithead in 1911, Louis saw him several times but only once alone. The Kaiser, warning that Britain must not tamper with Germany's relations with Russia, remarked arrogantly:

... You must be brought to understand in England that Germany is the sole arbiter of peace or war on the Continent. If we wish to fight [France] we will do so without your leave. And why? Because we Continental powers dispose of armies counting millions. Of what possible use would it be for you to land your 50,000 men anywhere? I am convinced you would never attempt anything so foolish, as those beautiful life guards and Grenadier Guards would be blown sky high by my submarines before they could set foot on shore. As to those French, we have beaten them once & we will beat them again. We know the road from Berlin to Paris. You know you can't mount your Dreadnoughts on wheels and come to your dear friends' assistance.

Prince Louis sent this detailed account of the Kaiser's invective to George v. In turn the King forwarded it in confidence to Winston Churchill, who disclosed the contents to the Foreign Secretary, Sir Edward Grey.

Ironically, although there would be wild accusations of pro-German sympathies, the British Government availed itself of Prince Louis's knowledge of matters concerning Germany and Russia. His prophecy of the German menace was now looming starkly. In readiness, he exercised his crews to the peak of efficiency and diligently worked at naval strategy. He also invented a new type of signalling apparatus. But at that juncture the antagonism in the Royal Navy also gave unease. A rival faction – 'the syndicate of discontent' – led by Lord Charles Beresford, vehemently attacked Fisher's reforms. Louis tended to support the First Sea Lord but not entirely without censure. Writing to Captain George King-Hall, he referred to his suggestion in 1907 to unite the Nore division of the Home Fleet, the Channel Fleet and the Atlantic Fleet into one command. Louis claimed that it would have been accepted but for Fisher's determination to prevent Beresford's taking command.

I think [wrote Louis] C.B. has been badly treated. ... You know how much I admire J.F. He is a truly great man, and almost all his schemes have benefited the Navy. But he has started this pernicious partisanship in the Navy – there is no denying it. Anyone who in any way opposed J.F. went under. His hatred of C.B. has led him to maintain for the past two years an organization of our Home forces which was indefensible and not adapted to war. This is so patent that everyone must see it, and constitutes a serious indictment.

The plan would be implemented only when Louis himself joined the Board of Admiralty. The threat of international strife – the *Agadir* crisis in the summer of 1911 – projected him to that seat of power. The French sent an expedition to Fez, a prelude to a move to annex Morocco. The Germans, in a counter-move, sent the gunboat *Panther* on the false pretext of protecting her nationals. It was more logical to assume that they were manoeuvring for a naval base on Africa's west coast to threaten British shipping to the Cape of Good Hope and South Africa.

On 23 August, as the crisis intensified, the British Government met to assess what could be done to aid France if attacked. 'The Cabinet', Lord Selborne exposed later, 'was shocked and amazed to find . . . that the Admiralty could produce no war plan for the Navy. It was so secret that only the First Sea Lord knew what it was! It was locked up in his brain!' Sir Arthur Wilson, who had succeeded Fisher as First Sea Lord in January 1910, was obsessed with the notion of one-man control, like his predecessor. Nothing had been done to create a Naval War Staff since Prince Louis had written his lengthy memorandum on the matter years earlier. Selborne further disclosed: 'I bequeathed that task as an urgent legacy to Fisher nearly seven years ago and gave him all the material for its fulfilment . . . I thought it would have been a job after his own heart, but obviously I was wrong.'

A drastic change was imperative. In 1911, the dynamic and brilliant Winston Churchill transferred from the Home Office to the Admiralty as First Lord, and was advised by Fisher, then living in Italy, to replace Wilson with Prince Louis. 'He (Battenberg) is the most capable administrator in the Admiral's list *by a long way*,' he wrote. Later, however, this contradictory man would condemn Louis as 'Winston's servile dupe'.

The appointment roused mixed and even biting comment due to Louis's German connections. 'Lloyd George', according to Lord Esher, 'was horrified at the idea of a German holding the supreme place. Asquith says L.G. is an excellent foolometer and that the public would take the same view. Still, he (Prince Louis) is the most competent man. . . .' Horatio Bottomley, in *John Bull*, ranted that it would be 'a crime against our Empire to trust our secrets of National Defence to any alien-born official. It is a heavy strain to put upon any German to make him a ruler of our Navy and give him the key to our defences . . .'

Despite the qualms, Prince Louis was appointed the Second Sea Lord, with Sir Francis Bridgeman in the senior capacity. Louis's star was in the ascendant. On relinquishing his sea command, he informed a friend that the Admiralty had just issued the 'long-expected addenda and alterations in the Signal Book. Its study was a great satisfaction to me, for the Admiralty have now adopted practically all the novelties I tried in the Atlantic Fleet, including my latest development of Cruiser Tactics. It certainly is a very great compliment to me.'

In December 1912, Sir Francis Bridgeman resigned through illness, and Prince Louis succeeded him. He continued to modernize the personnel and *matériel* of the navy, strategically reorganizing the Admiralty's internal administration and creating a war staff under Rear-Admiral Ernest Troubridge, whose urgent brief was to bring the fleets to a peak of readiness should an emergency arise. At Eastchurch areodrome, Louis helped to foster aviation – then in its infancy – totally ignorant that by the time his son Louis rose to senior rank, aircraft would render the new cherished dreadnoughts obsolete.

Ominous rumblings mounted in Europe in those fateful months of 1914, culminating in the assassination of the Archduke Franz Ferdinand of Austria and his wife at Sarajevo. On 24 July, Austro-Hungary ordered mobilization against Serbia. The next day – a Saturday – Prince Louis, sensing the proximity of crisis, stayed at his desk at the Admiralty. Churchill had left London, having chosen to visit his wife, who was convalescing at Cromer. Therefore any decisions that were to be made had to be made by Louis alone.

That month the Royal Navy's annual manoeuvres had recently concluded. For the first time in years nucleus crews of the reserve fleet had participated and were due to be discharged to their homes. Of that momentous weekend, Prince Louis wrote from his official residence, Mall House:

Ministers with their weekend holidays are incorrigible. Things looked pretty bad on Saturday, on which at 6 pm the [Austro-Hungary] ultimatum [to Serbia] expired. Asquith, Grey, Churchill and all the rest left London. I sat here all Sunday, reading all the telegrams from embassies as they arrived. On Monday morning the big fleet at Portland had orders to disperse, demobilize and give leave. I took it upon myself to countermand everything by telegraph on Sunday afternoon. When the Ministers hurried back late that evening, they cordially approved my action, and we had the drawn sword in our hands to back up our urgent advice. I breakfasted with the King on Monday morning to report the action taken.

The Kaiser's sword-rattling ceased. That day Austro-Hungary declared war. The First World War had begun. Prince Louis's intelligent action was scarcely that of a man with pro-German sympathies, yet some three months later, enemies would accuse him of being a German spy. Louis was swept up in a wave of national hatred towards things Germanic, naval reverses fortifying the anti-Battenberg campaign: the torpedoing of three ancient cruisers in the North Sea and the sinking of Admiral Sir Christopher Cradock's fleet at Coronel. Yet if Louis's earlier plans had been allowed to mature, it is reasonably certain that the cruisers *Hogue*, *Cressy* and *Aboukir* would not have been sunk by submarines. These vessels had occupied regular patrolling routes, now an antiquated practice which, as his war plan of 1913 revealed, Louis had opposed because of its vulnerability to the new menace – submerged craft.

Louis's intimate and biographer, Mark Kerr, claimed categorically that if the Prince, in August 1914, had not been worried by scandalous gossip, he would have stood out

Queen Ena of Spain with her children. Of the four sons, only one would escape
'the royal disease' – haemophilia. The scourge helped to undermine Bourbon
rule.

Prince Louis, then First Sea Lord of the Admiralty, with Winston
Churchill, the First Lord. Public hatred of things Germanic compelled
Prince Louis to resign from office.

against the advice urged upon him by the chief of the war staff and others – 'for on the day they [the cruisers] were sunk, he observed to one of his staff: "I should not have given in to them." ' But the public, full of hate, was ignorant of the Admiralty's inner workings. Rumours multiplied and vied in exaggeration – 'sighting' U-boats lurking in coves and river mouths around the coast. Irresponsible tongues claimed that someone in the Admiralty was engaged in nefarious intrigue with the Germans. And on 3 October, Fisher noted: 'One of the queer canards that are flying round London is that Prince Louis of Battenberg, First Sea Lord of the Admiralty, is confined in the Tower of London.' Fisher knew how fatuous this was, but he now held the inflexible view that Britain's naval difficulties stemmed from his belief that 'our directing Sea Lord [is] played out'.

This was yet another of Fisher's baseless and erratic statements considering that, on the day he wrote his letter, the cabinet had empowered Prince Louis with total responsibility at the Admiralty during Churchill's visit to Antwerp. But the innuendoes persisted. At a London club, Louis put on a jocular yet false façade when a member asked: 'What are you doing here, Admiral? I thought you were in the Tower.' 'You're behind the times, old man,' Louis remarked humorously, 'I was shot last Thursday.'

As on other occasions, Lord Charles Beresford led a vindictive coterie who clamoured for Louis's dismissal. At the Carlton Club, according to Arthur Lee, a future First Lord, Beresford 'expressed the opinion that *all* Germans including highly placed ones, ought to leave the country as they were in close touch with Germans abroad'. Referring to Prince Louis, Beresford argued that, despite his skill as an officer, 'nothing could alter the fact that he is a *German*, and as such should not be occupying his present position. He keeps German servants and has his property in Germany.' Most contemptible of all was the despicable claim that they had read 'a letter from Germany, revealing that Prince Louis was a German spy'. So fanatical and defamatory had the accusations become that Churchill, it is claimed, threatened to obstruct Beresford's ambition to be appointed an Admiral of the Fleet (retired).

Mark Kerr asserted that Admiral of the Fleet Lord John Hay had been clever enough to guess that German propaganda was being used by 'idiotic gossips to discredit Prince Louis in the eyes of the public'. In a letter to *The Times*, Lord Hay wrote: 'The ingeniously propagated lies as to the Russian troops from Archangel have died out, and we are now provided with a new sensation. We have all of us heard the muttering of slander about Prince Louis of Battenberg. It has now been raised from the gutter ... as conversation in small coteries by a pronouncement ... in one of the ablest of the evening newspapers.'

Tragically, the tide of suspicion could not be dammed. Many letters to the press disclosed that the writers never doubted Prince Louis's patriotism, but the contents could be crystallized in the comment that, due to his German origin, he was incapable of that animosity which the British wanted the head of the navy to possess at that critical juncture. Correspondence deteriorated, however, into ridiculous charges of treason. The strain on Prince Louis was formidable. 'My responsibility and constant anxiety in this great office are heavy,' he wrote to Lord Walter Kerr on 26 October, 'and being continuously attacked and yet quite helpless – although assured afresh of the Government's confidence – and I feel sometimes that I cannot bear it much longer.'

On the same day, an editorial in *The Globe* affirmed confidence in Prince Louis's integrity but at the same time asked for some unequivocal statement to be issued, which would dispel the doubts and rumours once and for all. But no statement was forthcoming. Churchill, distrusted by his colleagues in the Asquith government, was struggling for his own political survival. Even on 27 October, when the new dreadnought *Audacious* struck a German mine in the Irish Sea, it was believed that Prince Louis was about to be sacrificed on the political altar. This is confirmed somewhat by the Prime Minister's notes written the next day: 'The sinking of the *Audacious* ... is cruel luck for Winston, who has just been here pouring out his woes ... Winston's real trouble, however, is about Prince Louis ... He must go, and Winston has had a most painful interview with him. Louis behaved with great dignity and public spirit and will resign at once.'

Did Churchill bear for years a sense of guilt? His willingness to advance the career of Prince Louis's younger son, Lord Louis Mountbatten, in the Second World War suggests that perhaps he did.

On that unforgettable day, Prince Louis wrote a letter to Churchill saying that he had 'lately been driven to the painful conclusion that ... my birth and parentage have the effect of impairing ... my usefulness on the Board of Admiralty. In these circumstances I feel it to be my duty, as a loyal subject of His Majesty, to resign the office of First Sea Lord, hoping thereby to facilitate the task of the administration of the great Service, to which I have devoted my life...' (Ironically, on the same day Louis's nephew, Prince Maurice of Battenberg, was killed in the bloody battle at Ypres.)

Accepting the resignation, Churchill replied:

The Navy of today, and still more the Navy of tomorrow, bears the imprint of your work. The enormous impending influx of capital ships, the score of thirty-knot cruisers, the destroyers and submarines unequalled in modern construction which are coming now to hand, are the results of labours which ... the Board of Admiralty owes so much to your aid.

The first step which secured the timely concentration of the fleet was taken by you ... The spirit in which you have acted is the same in which Prince Maurice of Battenberg has given his life to our cause and in which your gallant son [George] is now serving in the fleet.

The next day King George V entered in his diary that he had spent a most

trying day ... At 11.30 saw Winston Churchill who informed me that Louis of Battenberg had resigned ... The press and public have said so many things against him being born a German ... I feel deeply for him: there is no more loyal man in the country...

At 4.01 saw poor Louis, very painful interview, he quite broke down. I told him I would make him a Privy Councillor to show the confidence I had in him, which pleased him.

Somewhat incongruously, after the resignation praise came flooding in. Prince Louis's services were a real loss to the nation. With hindsight, it is apparent that if he had remained in office, Britain's naval warfare would have been fought with greater strategy. In particular, the convoy system – obviating the loss of many ships, cargoes and lives – would have been built up sooner to counter the U-boat menace.

He retired with dignity to Kent House on the Isle of Wight. Quietly he devoted time to Red Cross activities and embarked on an extensive history of naval medals which was completed by his son, Lord Louis Mountbatten, after his death.

The latter years of Prince Louis's life were overshadowed by the deaths of the Romanoffs. In 1905, Louis's brother-in-law, the Grand Duke Serge, husband of his wife's sister Ella, had resigned from the Governor-Generalship of Moscow, displeased with what he claimed to be the Tsar's pusillanimous policy. On that February day, the snow was melting and crashing from the rooftops as Serge was returning to his office to collect his personal belongings. Suddenly, in the cold air, there was a terrifying noise: the Nihilists had struck again, and the Grand Duke lay dead.

Ella, his widow, the Grand Duchess with gargantuan wealth, now founded a religious nursing order, the only one in Russia, devoting the rest of her life to her Convent of Martha and Mary where, living humbly near by, and wearing a grey robe and white veil, she and her nuns ministered to the needs of the poor and sick of Moscow. Princess Victoria frequently visited her sisters until the First World War made it impossible. In July 1912, accompanied by Nona Kerr, her lady-in-waiting, she occupied rooms in a modest little house beside Ella's convent, but were so tormented by bugs that after the first night they took refuge with Ella.

That summer was exceptionally torrid in Russia – rather in keeping with the mood of Victoria's hypochondriac and neurotic sister, the Tsarina Alicky. The strain of Court life, the chronic anxiety occasioned by her haemophiliac son, and her mystical religious character, were destroying her. In desperation she had grown to rely increasingly on Rasputin, the *staretz*, or wandering holy man. 'Alexandra Feodorovna', wrote one of the Tsarina's ladies-in-waiting, 'spoke of herself as a "great worrier", and this was true, but when anxieties gained the upper hand, Rasputin's pious outpourings and her faith in his prayers and prophesies gave her confidence. The Emperor found a certain peace of mind in the hopeful assurances that in the end all would go well, and was glad to see the comfort the Empress derived from her trust in Rasputin's healing powers.'

To Victoria's dismay, a rift – due to Rasputin's influence – had widened between her and her sister. After leaving Ella in Moscow, Victoria stayed with Alicky at Peterhof in August. There was not merely the haunting fear of haemophilia but also the threat of anarchy.

Victoria never truly bridged the gap between her sisters, but to her joy there was yet another 'Russian invasion' at Heiligenberg during the following summer. Together with their children, the Battenbergs, the Romanoffs, and Andrew and Alice of Greece met, before most of Europe's ruling dynasties vanished in the reeking ashes of Armageddon. The future Earl Mountbatten was there, then only thirteen, and smitten with calf love for his cousin, Marie of Russia. There were parties, picnics and dancing. 'There we were together – just one great family like any other family.'

With her daughter Louise and Nona Kerr, Victoria again travelled to Russia in the summer of 1914. Ella was also there, and they steamed in the imperial yacht from Nijni Novgorod (now Gorky) down the Volga. Two places at which they called would have immense portent. On reaching Perm, the party split up, Ella visiting the convent at Alapaevsk, where four years later the Bolsheviks would incarcerate her in the local school-house then brutally kill her. Princess Victoria and her companions, by a curious stroke of fate, set out on a journey of equal historical significance. Crossing the Urals, they came to Ekaterinburg, an ugly mining town. Victoria noted a sense of hostility beneath the veneer of formality. Eventually she wrote that 'the population did not seem particularly pleased at the official visit. I noticed it, especially, at an evening entertainment of fireworks, where the crowd was quite unenthusiastic.' As she passed through the centre of the town, she was attracted by a big house that dominated the square. Four years later that plain building would figure sombrely as the death scene where, in the basement, the Bolsheviks would annihilate the imperial family.

Victoria's Russian visit almost separated her from Prince Louis throughout the war. At Ekaterinburg a message from him warned his wife of the impending conflict. Because Louis and Nona Kerr were both suffering from a severe throat infection, the party hurried first to St Petersburg, where the Winter Palace, now closed for the summer, was re-opened for them. But there was no time to waste. Risks abounded. Already fierce fighting had broken out on Russia's western borders. In their haste Princess Victoria sacrificed her jewels, but Alicky fitted out the party with warm clothes and presented each with a little bag of gold sovereigns which they secreted in their dresses. A special train conveyed them to the Russian frontier at Torneo at the head of the Gulf of Bothnia.

Other relatives were speeding homewards. Shunted into a frontier siding, Princess Victoria was amazed to see 'Aunt Minnie', the widow of the ill-fated Tsar Alexander III, and her daughter Olga Alexandrovna in a nearby carriage.

With the aid of a British Embassy official, Victoria assisted the two invalids over a wooden footbridge connecting Russia and Sweden. Only one train was due to leave for Stockholm, but every seat had already been occupied by officials of the Austrian Embassy in St Petersburg. At the cost of £75 in gold, the Swedish authorities were induced to couple on the carriage which the Dowager Empress Minnie and her daughter had so lately vacated.

Louise and Victoria never saw their Russian relatives again. Moreover, during the war years news was scarce. As would be learned later, Rasputin tightened his grip on the Romanoffs and freely expressed enmity to the war. He had been introduced to the Tsarina by Anna Alexandrovna Virubova, daughter of the Director of the Private

Chancellery of His Majesty, and in *The Secret Journal of Anna Virubova*, the entry for 15 August 1915 reveals: ' "I can't give my blessing to this war," said the staretz ... "Papa [the Tsar] got out of the Japanese War with nothing worse than a carbuncle, but this time it will be a wound that will never heal. The war is the enemy that is killing us all!" '

This publication is claimed to be spurious, but it is hard to say, for rumours run rife, and it is often hard to sort fact from fiction. Rasputin's hostility may have provoked Allied anger. It was said that, paid by secretly pro-German bankers, he and the Tsarina were in collusion to betray the Imperial Army. But although Alicky was a German, she was a German of Hesse and not of Prussia. Indeed, her loathing for the Kaiser is apparent in this account of her outburst, of 19 December 1914, in the *Virubova Journal*: 'If by hating one could set on fire, I would burn up even the memory of that hateful Emperor William! ... And people suspect me of wanting to deliver Russia to this august representative of Germany!'

After their first house-arrest, the imperial family was removed from Tsarskoe-Selo to Tobolsk – by a coincidence not far from Rasputin's place of birth. Even before the Bolsheviks had wrested power from Kerensky's government, the prisoners suffered humiliation; the behaviour of uncouth guards deteriorated into sadism. Towards the end of April 1918, as the White Armies of Admiral Kolchak began to close in, the Tsar and his family were transported to Ekaterinburg – the final journey supervised by Comrade Sverdlov, a Jew, who, christened 'the Red Tsar', had vowed to obliterate the imperial family.

Through an intermediary, Princess Victoria pleaded with Lenin's wife for mercy for her relatives. She actually persuaded her nephew, the neutral King of Spain, to offer refuge to her sister and her children if released. But her pleas were futile. Lenin was unrelenting.

Trotsky later admitted that the ghastly executions were ordered by Lenin, with the approval of Sverdlov and himself. The imperial family were shot on the night of 16–17 July in the basement of the house which had roused Princess Victoria's attention four years earlier – the home of an engineer named Ipatiev, who had fled. Not content with murdering the imperial family and cutting off the fingers of, almost certainly, the Tsarina for the sake of her rings, the butchers even killed a particularly lovely dog belonging to one of the Grand Duchesses. A quantity of small objects in the upstairs room, such as torn or charred fragments of letters and photographs, ikons shorn of their jewels, medicine bottles, prayer-books, work baskets and simple articles of toilet were taken away by the *Juge d'instruction*, Sokolov, appointed by Kolchak to inquire into all the details of the murders. There were also locks of hair belonging to the Grand Duchesses when they were babies, which the Tsarina had carried with her on her last and most fearful journey.

Ella's fate was, if anything, more gruesome. On 18 July a lorry stopped outside the school-house at Alapaevsk where Ella and others were being detained. Ordered by guards to get on board, the party was driven into the countryside that was aglow with the evening sun. Ella and Prince John started to sing the Magnificat, then the others sang too. Next came the notes of *Sviete Tikhiy* ('Hail, Gentle Light').

Passing through a forest 'fragrant with mushrooms and wild strawberries', the lorry stopped eventually in an exposed area fringed with trees to the east. Less than fifty yards ahead gaped the opening of a dark, disused mine-shaft. It was all too apparent what the guards proposed to do. The Grand Duke Serge Michailovitch struggled so furiously that he was shot, yet he was still alive when he was flung into the mine. One by one, on that gilded evening, the prisoners vanished into the gloom of the shaft. Kneeling at the edge of the pit, with the guards clutching her shoulders, Ella loudly asked God to forgive their executioners. As the last victim made the terrible descent, the guards, as a ghastly finale, hurled down hand-grenades into the darkness.

Although badly injured, some of the victims must have survived for a while, for it is said that throughout the night and the next day peasants heard chanting rising from the depths of the shaft. Then there was silence.

Maybe Ella did not die immediately, for, when the bodies were recovered, it was seen that part of her habit had been torn off to bandage Prince John's right arm, perhaps broken by the fall. Some days later, White Russian troops arrived, and the bodies were brought up from the mine. In the neighbourhood, there was a monk named Father Seraphim, the son of a Moscow merchant, who regarded Ella as a saint. He vowed that the bodies of the Grand Duchess and Sister Barbara, the faithful companion who had died with her, should be taken to Palestine.

In 1920, Princess Beatrice chanced upon a newspaper illustration of intense interest; it depicted a little shrine in a chapel in Shanghai; here, it was claimed, were coffins containing the bodies of Ella and her loyal maid. Enquiries proved the veracity of the tale, and the bodies were brought to Jerusalem for burial in the Russian church built outside the Damascus Gate. There Prince Louis and Princess Victoria, with their daughter Louise, listened to a remarkable story. Father Seraphim, Louis subsequently revealed, had sealed the bodies 'in lead coffins, and brought them gradually and with immense difficulty all the way from Siberia and Manchuria to Peking, to the Russian Chapel there. And then on 1 December he brought the two coffins (enclosed in beautifully-made Chinese wooden coffins mounted with brass) with the help of two assistants, from Peking by train to Tientsin, from there by coastal steamer to Shanghai and thence by ocean steamer to Hong Kong, Colombo, and Bombay to Port Said.'

With his wife and daughter, Louis met Father Seraphim at Port Said. 'This good priest,' wrote Louis, 'a Messianic looking man with long hair and a beard', had kept the coffins in his custody for two and a half years. Writing to Princess Beatrice from the Grand New Hotel, Jerusalem, on 29 January 1921, Louis explained:

Yesterday we deposited the precious remains in the beautiful Chapel (in memory of my Aunt Marie) on the Mount of Olives ... On the lid (of Ella's coffin) was let in a framed photograph of Ella and brass Slav Cross. At the head end a silver plate with a long Russian inscription. The good priest ... who ... smuggled them (the bodies) by degrees out of Siberia into China ... and his two assistants ... are going to remain there. The two coffins are going to be walled up in a portion of the vault under the church, and a small chapel will be fitted up in the outer open vaults, which communicate, by a window, with a Mortuary Chamber.

The brutal deaths of the Romanoffs, and the mental scars left by slanderous tongues, spread a blight over Prince Louis's final years, and perhaps shortened his life. Happily, two events gave him enormous joy. On 21 July 1921, he was invited to preside at the Navy Club dinner in London. The ovation was tremendous. The other – very close to his death – was his appointment as Admiral of the Fleet on the retired list. He and his wife and daughter Louise lived somewhat frugally on his pension of £2,000 a year. Indeed, it was for financial reasons that he had to quit Kent House. For a while they resided at Fishponds, a charming house near Netley in Hampshire, owned by Colonel Richard Crichton, who had married Nona Kerr. Considering his social status, life for Louis was now essentially modest. Seeing him outside the United Services Club (so one story goes), a contemporary offered him his taxi. Thanking him, Louis replied: 'Oh, no, my dear fellow, I go in buses these days.'

During July 1921, he joined his son Louis – then serving with the Home Fleet – in a cruise in the *Repulse* and returned to London to arrange a visit to Constantinople to his elder son George, now gunnery lieutenant in the *Cardiff*. But first he intended to journey to Scotland: hence the hiring of a room at the Naval and Military Club in London's Half Moon Street, while his wife and daughter stayed at a hotel close by. On Saturday, 10 September, feeling unwell, Prince Louis delayed departure. The next day Princess Victoria and Louise went to buy medicine, but it was too late. A tearful housekeeper broke the news on their return: she had gone to Prince Louis's room to collect a tray and found him dead.

Although Prince Louis was not affluent by royal standards, Princess Victoria – now occupying a grace-and-favour apartment at Kensington Palace – was not left in dire straits. She had lost all her jewellery in Russia, and the deprivation of a valuable holding in a Russian platinum mine had depleted their income further; Louis sold Heiligenberg after the war for £30,000, much of which vanished with the dramatic devaluation of the mark. However, years earlier Louis had invented the 'Battenberg Course Indicator', which is used in the world's navies to this day. When a committee was founded to reward those whose inventions had contributed to victory, Louis's ardent friend, Admiral Mark Kerr, applied for a grant, unknown to Victoria. But when the news was broached to her, she stubbornly declined all forms of payment, even her pension as a widow of an Admiral of the Fleet. She had inherited money from her mother. There remained almost £30,000 when her will was proved in 1951.

8

Setting the Life-Style

WHILE hysterical anti-German prejudice was at high pitch in Britain during the First World War, 'Dickie' of Battenberg wrote from Osborne to Princess Victoria, his mother, that

Papa has turned out to be a German spy and has been discreetly marched off to the Tower ... Apparently the rumour started (outside the college of course) by the fact that an admiral or somebody has been recalled from the Mediterranean to find out about the *Goeben* & *Breslau* escaping. People apparently think he let the German cruiser escape as he was a spy or an agent ... I got a rather rotten time of it for about three days as little fools ... insisted on calling me German Spy & kept on heckling me & trying to make things unpleasant for me ...

Jingoism and public anxiety that the Battenbergs' sympathy for their native land was deep seated could not be wholly condemned. In peacetime, neither Louis nor Victoria had done anything to allay those fears. Prince Louis, indeed, had actually suspected that if war erupted his situation might be untenable. Maybe Queen Victoria had entertained similar thoughts; at least she had strongly advised the Battenbergs to take up permanent residence in England. Instead, they had lived much in Hesse, rooted in Heiligenberg. Prince Louis had once contemplated selling his German estate, until the Grand Duke of Hesse pleaded with him to refrain from severing himself completely from his German connection.

In her own particular way, the outspoken Victoria was also partly responsible for her husband's downfall. She was not always tactful, although she could not have been more absolutely English and patriotic. She exercised a strong influence over Prince Louis's professional life, and was invaluable to him because she knew a great deal about the German navy because she was sister-in-law to Prince Henry of Prussia. But because she communicated her information to a large number of people, one could not help but speculate about what she would be saying about the British navy when she went to Germany.

If it is true that Princess Victoria unwittingly undermined her husband's career, by the same token her actions innocently created a challenge in life for Dickie, her son. The story has been told – and it has since been confirmed by Earl Mountbatten himself

– that when he was informed at Osborne of his father's resignation, he walked alone to the flagstaff, standing to attention with tears streaming down his cheeks. Until then Dickie had been somewhat lethargic, a cadet of mediocre attainments, a poor comparison when set against the brilliance of his brother George. In fact, in those days there was little to predict his future as Admiral of the Fleet, or the dynamism he showed in the Second World War as Chief of Combined Operations and Supreme Allied Commander in South-East Asia. Neither were there signs of the keen imagination and willpower that he would need as the last Viceroy of the Indian sub-continent, as the architect of the modern Royal Navy, and as the man who, amid much criticism, caused what was tantamount to a revolution in Britain's system of defence.

Dickie, a great-grandson of Queen Victoria, was born on 25 June 1900. He would be the ageing matriarch's last godchild and, despite the fact that he knocked off her spectacles after his christening at Frogmore, she recorded: 'He is a beautiful large child and behaved very well.' The baptism was more significant for the misery which it brought Dr Elliott, the Dean of Windsor, who conducted the ceremony. The heat, which the old Queen found oppressive, was overbearing on that summer afternoon. To try to assuage the discomfort, buckets of ice were placed about the room, one standing beneath the chair occupied for a while by the Dean. Much too late he felt the freezing chill in his legs; the ensuing sciatic inflammation crippled him for life.

The child received the names Albert Victor Nicholas Louis Francis, and at first he was nicknamed 'Nickie' until, to avoid confusion with the Tsar, it was changed to 'Dickie'. In his earlier years, due to the nomadic life of his parents, Dickie's world was cosmopolitan. But the prevailing atmosphere was of fighting ships and the crews who manned them. In early childhood he was the unofficial mascot of his father's flagship, and on visits to Kiel he roamed about German men-of-war with Prince Henry of Prussia, his sailor uncle. Doodling warships would grow into a habit which he shared with the Kaiser. As in the case of his brother George, there was never any question as to the career he would choose.

Dickie was ten when he went as a boarder for three years to Locker's Park, an exclusive preparatory school in Hertfordshire. Princess Victoria wrote often, offering advice. It is clear that he missed his parents, certainly in the early stages, for his mother wrote: 'All one's life is made up of pain & pleasure, meeting & parting & I have always tried not to let my mind dwell on the sad things ... otherwise one's heart aches too much. You must try to do the same ...'

As Prince Louis had experienced during his early days in the navy, Dickie's bugbear at this period was the French master who, for no apparent reason, treated him unreasonably. Dickie's accomplishments, however, in both studies and sports, were only modest, and when he proceeded to the Royal Naval College, he passed out only thirty-fifth in a class of eighty. But did the disturbing environment of Osborne militate against him? Curiously, his social rank as a cousin of the reigning King made him the butt of much bullying. 'All my term greatly pity me,' he revealed to his parents, 'because

I have ... been asked over a hundred times my name, whether I was a prince, our cook's name (the only thing I refuse) etc. I get pointed at, have my cap knocked off ... However, I am now so used to this that I don't mind it much.' Admiral Sir Percy Scott's son learned the painful way not to dislodge the Mountbatten cap. Dickie gave him a beating, and his prestige soared. But the hostility went on, and, after a year at Osborne, he wrote to his mother: 'I have only got one real chum left now, Graham. Stopford got so ragged at being chums with me that he has chucked it ...'

Yet from this time there was a great change. The disgrace which Prince Louis had suffered transformed him into a son determined to eradicate the slander which had been disgracefully attributed to his father. On transferring to Dartmouth he rose to eighteenth place out of eighty, and in a special three-month course at Devonport – a substitute for the usual six months in a training cruiser in peacetime – he became leading cadet.

These boyhood scenes were an indication of the future: controversy would flare up around him time and again, as it had around his father and their Battenberg relations. In later years the cynics would scoff at the gilded playboy. They would admit that he was the ideal companion in a thorny predicament but add that no one was more adept at creating such a situation. In due course, irate Tories would rage over the 'Viceroy of Scuttle'. However, no matter how one views him, Earl Mountbatten has etched his graphic personality on his times. Born during the declining years of European monarchy, he has skilfully adapted himself to the drastic changes wrought by social revolution. His detractors accuse him of being little more than an opportunist carefully exploiting rank, affluence and people of influence. Yet it is more realistic to visualize a person of liberal policies driven onwards by an inexorable force.

Lord Louis has epitomized to the full the Mountbatten talent for appearing in spectacular situations. His career is marked by the occupational hazards of the unquiet mind. It is a story of action, not introspection, and exhibits such a juxtaposition of opposing qualities that it is difficult to get a clear picture of the man. The polo-playing aristocrat appears side-by-side with the radical-minded proconsul, the princely sprig of sheltered birth with the fighting-mad destroyer captain, the Viceroy inspired by the broad sweep of momentous events with the querulous and demanding bureaucrat absorbed in infinitesimal detail. As if his own personality was not replete with sufficient fascination, he looms large in the public mind as the uncle and mentor of the progenitor of our future kings and queens, Prince Philip.

As a midshipman, in 1916 he served under Admiral David Beatty, first in the *Lion* and then in the *Queen Elizabeth*. To his regret, he never participated in the Battle of Jutland, but, joining the *Lion* when she came out of dock after that action, there was still excitement, on 19 August. The German fleet put to sea again and then dashed back to port.

I was on the bridge at the time [wrote Louis], attending to the captain [Chatfield] & he told me to report to the engine room, 'Will probably be opening fire in 15 or 20 minutes time.' We sighted 5 or 6 Zeppelins who gave us away & prevented an action. Our seaplane carrier sent up a seaplane & one of our light cruisers opened fire. Five minutes after going off watch, one of our screen, the *Nottingham*, was 'moulied' (attacked by torpedoes) & on our return, the *Lowestoft* went up (another of our screen), about ten minutes before I went on watch. We had three 'moulies' miss us on the way back, and every BC [battle cruiser] had 2 or 3 fired at them.

While drinking tea in the gun-room, the midshipmen dashed up on deck after the *Lion* heeled over. The ship was in the middle of 'a minefield laid for our benefit, and while we were still altering course to avoid mines, a torpedo was fired that missed us by a matter of feet'.

Eventually Lord Louis served in a submarine of the K6 class, and at the Armistice – then a sub-lieutenant and eighteen years old – he was second in command of P31, a small escort vessel operating in the English Channel.

The first year of peace he spent at Christ's College, Cambridge, under an Admiralty arrangement for young officers of his age. His mother wrote explaining that she expected the 'horrible wrench it will be to give up your beloved P31'. Wrench or not, Lord Louis's life at Cambridge was decidedly lively. Two companions were King George v's sons, Prince Albert (the future George VI) and Prince Henry, and all three were admitted to the Union.

In his second term Lord Louis led a debate against Oxford, and proposed the motion 'that the time is ripe for a Labour Government'. Winston Churchill, then War Minister in Lloyd George's coalition government, agreed to support him. Lord Louis astonished the Union when, addressing himself to the president, he remarked: 'Sir, in my humble opinion everything that has been said so far by the speakers on both sides is tripe.'

From now onwards, Lord Mountbatten's life would at times bear an uncanny resemblance to that of his father. Returning from a tour of Canada and the United States in December 1919, the Prince of Wales now awaited a voyage to the West Indies, Australia and New Zealand in the spring: Mountbatten had an insatiable desire to accompany him. But whereas the future Edward VII had personally instigated the invitation to Prince Louis, Lord Louis had to rely entirely on his wits to gain one. Aware that the Prince of Wales was attending a London ball given by Lady Ribblesdale, Lord Louis arranged through a friend to be present as well, and the royal invitation was given.

Mountbatten was on board as the Prince's aide-de-camp when the battleship *Renown* embarked on the seven-month cruise. For the second time in the Battenberg family, it was the birth of an intimate friendship with the heir to the throne. It would endure even the vicissitudes of the abdication. Lord Louis's personality so endeared itself to the Prince that he was asked to fulfil similar duties on a tour of India and Japan the following year. Meanwhile, and again emulating his father, Lord Louis immersed himself wholeheartedly in the London season. At one of the events – a ball arranged by the American hostess Mrs Cornelius Vanderbilt – he met someone who would drastically mould his future way of life. Her name was Edwina Ashley, and she was the grand-daughter of one of the wealthiest men of the day – Sir Ernest Cassel.

Sir Ernest Cassel was born on 3 March 1852 in Cologne, the youngest child of Jacob Cassel, a Jewish money-lender and small private banker. The brilliance of his mind was first conveyed as a child prodigy at chess. Because the family concern was too small to absorb him, Ernest was apprenticed to the firm of Elzbacher & Co, in Cologne, with prospects of promotion to ledger clerk. For Ernest such financial horizons were too distant and bleak. Therefore, when sixteen years old, he arrived in Liverpool as an immi-grant, with a small number of clothes and his violin, then secured a clerkship with Blessig, Braun & Cox, grain merchants of German origin. Flimsy evidence purports that he first received fifteen shillings a week, but this Sir Ernest would deny years later, remarking: 'I never got less than two pounds a week. I was not so cheap as all that.' Living with a kindly widow, he rose at 6.30 every morning to walk from his little dark room to save the penny fare on the horse-trams. Evenings were invariably devoted to learning English, either from a borrowed primer or by attending classes at the Mechanical Institute, where immigrants were taught for a fee of threepence.

A year spent as a clerk in the Anglo-Egyptian Bank in Paris saw the beginning of the financial trek that took him to multi-millionaire status. Cassel escaped the siege of Paris of 1870–71 but before he quit the city he had won the admiration of another Jew of humble origin like himself, Moritz Hirsch, at thirty one of Europe's greatest financiers. Born in Munich, Hirsch had received concessions from the Ottoman Empire in Egypt and the Middle East and, emerging as the foremost banker of the Austro-Hungarian Empire, was created a baron in 1869 by the Emperor Francis Joseph. Railways in the Balkans and Turkey were the product of his acumen. His financial ramifications were wide.

Impressed by young Cassel, Hirsch recommended him to his brother-in-law Louis Bischoffsheim, the senior partner of the London finance house of Bischoffsheim & Goldschmidt. From the moment that he arrived at their Bishopsgate office, Cassel's financial stature grew to phenomenal proportions in both Europe and the United States. After Cassel had rescued a firm from ruin in Constantinople, and at the same time safeguarded Bischoffsheim and other City investments, Louis Bischoffsheim offered him a salary of £500, but Cassel immediately replied: 'You mean, of course, £5,000?' Bischoffsheim readily acquiesced.

Cassel, then thirty-two, severed his connection with Bischoffsheim in 1884, occupy-ing an office at 21, Old Broad Street. A brass plate at the entrance merely announced: 'E. Cassel, First Floor'. This was his sole ostensible link with the outside world until he retired a multi-millionaire, even though his offices eventually occupied a multi-storey building.

Dealing with a group of Jewish bankers on both sides of the Atlantic, among his many interests were railways in the United States, tramways and livestock in Argentina,

canals, land irrigation, coffee and tin in South America, railways and ore mining in
Sweden, banking in Turkey, railways in the Balkans, and the development of the
dominions of the Ottoman Empire. He was identified with men of vast political power,
such as Lord Cromer, then the uncrowned ruler of Egypt. But it was the death of Baron
Hirsch in 1896 that took Cassel to the apogee of power. Hirsch, who had appointed
Cassel the executor of his tremendous estate, had been a close financial adviser of the
Prince of Wales, and Cassel succeeded him. Introduced to the Prince at a race meeting,
he would exceed his predecessor's royal connections, for whereas Hirsch had been one
of a circle of intimates, Ernest Cassel would become the future Edward VII's most
important friend. It was a curious relationship between personalities of arrestingly
different backgrounds, character and approach to life.

Prince Louis of Battenberg was another stalwart of the Marlborough House set, but
there is no evidence that he and Cassel were even companions. Socially, in those times,
Battenberg and Cassel were poles apart. To the old dynasties men like Cassel, in spite
of their fantastic riches, were of lower caste. But the two men symbolized changing
times. The ancient social hierarchies were in a state of decline; Cassel and the new
fraternity of international financiers were coming into their own, opening up the great
commercial enterprises abroad and injecting new prosperity into Britain.

The Prince of Wales, deprived by the Queen of his rightful place in state affairs,
and dissipating his energies in worldly pleasures, revelled in such company, deliberately
flouting the social barriers that had debarred men like Cassel from higher society. The
Queen disapproved. Even the Prince's nephew, the Kaiser, expressed resentment,
claiming that his uncle's mode of life showered disgrace on his colonelship in the
Prussian Hussars.

Queen Victoria objected to some of her heir's companions for specific reasons. She
disliked self-made men, and she disapproved equally of Americans and Jews. 'To make
a *Jew a Peer* is a step the Queen *could not* consent to,'she once wrote to Lord Granville.
She did not believe that a man who owed his wealth to contracts with foreign governments for loans, or to successful speculation on the Stock Exchange could fairly claim
a British peerage. After several abortive attempts, the Prince finally persuaded his
reluctant mother to make Cassel a Knight of the Order of St Michael and St George,
not for his services to the Prince but for those to the Queen and her government in
Egyptian affairs. When on the throne Edward VII would make Cassel a Privy Councillor,
awarding him the Grand Cross of the Victorian Order in 1906 and the Grand Cross
of the Order of the Bath three years later.

Sir Ernest Cassel knew great wealth and immense personal grief. His mother, to
whom he was devoted, died in her prime in 1874. Within the year, his father and brother
Max were dead. His younger sister Minnie and himself were the only surviving members
of his family.

His marriage was marked by tragedy. Sir Ernest first met his future wife, Annette
Maxwell, a frail member of a middle-class family, in Darlington, at one of the rare

After her husband had been assassinated, the Grand Duchess Serge (Ella of Hesse) founded an order which attended to the poor and the sick. Like other members of the imperial family, she was murdered by the Bolsheviks.

The financier, Sir Ernest Cassel, an intimate of Edward VII. The major part of his vast fortune was inherited by his grand-daughter, Edwina Ashley, the wife of Earl Mountbatten of Burma.

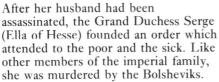

The wedding of Lord Louis Mountbatten and Miss Edwina Ashley was attended by King George V and Queen Mary and many other members of the British and European aristocracy.

social functions that he attended. A delicate child, Maud, was born eighteen months after the marriage, but she remembered little of her mother; Annette succumbed to tuberculosis. Before she died in her husband's arms, she implored him to change his faith. Sir Ernest, who had previously opposed this, now readily consented, aware of the joy his wife would derive in her final hours. For the woman he genuinely loved, Sir Ernest sacrificed his Jewish traditions and studied Catholic dogma under the guidance of a Jesuit priest, but he kept his conversion secret.

The wealth and care which he would have lavished on his wife was now bestowed upon his daughter. It seems certain that he was determined to marry her into nobility. The year 1901 was significant. Cassel's royal friend acceded to the throne as Edward VII, and later that year his daughter Maud married Wilfred Ashley. His son-in-law's status ranked high in the social hierarchy as a grandson of the eminent reformer, the seventh Earl of Shaftesbury, whose wife was the niece of Lord Melbourne, the Victorian Prime Minister. This female ancestor of Wilfred Ashley married as her second husband Lord Palmerston, whose estates, including Broadlands, duly passed into the Ashley family.

The world seemed to lie at Sir Ernest's feet. When his grand-daughter Edwina was born, King Edward stood sponsor at her baptism. And to enhance his place in society, in 1905 he acquired a grandiose mansion – Brook House in Park Lane. But four years later his domestic world crumbled again; Maud, susceptible to tuberculosis like her mother, was doomed to die. Desperately trying to prolong her life, Sir Ernest took her to Egypt and Switzerland, hiring complete hotels to secure peace and buying an estate in the Swiss Alps.

Before Maud Ashley's death, King Edward VII died on 6 May 1910. It is proof of his profound friendship that, among all the people that he knew, the King should send for his financier friend in his last hours. Writing to Maud, Sir Ernest described that final meeting, explaining:

He looked as if he had suffered great pain, and spoke indistinctly. His kindly smile came out as he congratulated me on having you brought home so much improved in health. He said, 'I am very seedy, but I wanted to see you ...' He then talked about other matters, and I had to ask his leave to go as I felt it was not good for him to go on speaking ... Sir James Reid told me he had dressed on purpose to receive me, and they could not stop him.

After Maud Ashley died in March 1911, Sir Ernest Cassel led a reclusive life amid the vast opulence of Brook House. The final shattering blow was the First World War. Through his friend Albert Ballin, the head of the Hamburg-America line, and German industrialists and bankers, Cassel had striven to ease the strained relations between Britain and Germany. Edward VII had thanked him but had remained obdurate in his detestation of German militarism and imperial aspirations. Cassel's sincere efforts proved abortive, much to his dismay.

Ernest Cassel, who had become naturalized at the time of his marriage, now encountered the same fate as Prince Louis of Battenberg. As the guns began to blast in Europe, tongues – including those of people who had enjoyed his sumptuous hospitality in peacetime – accused him of treachery. Though tacitly, some members of the British cabinet, including Asquith, the Prime Minister, remained quite amicable and even requested him to become an economic adviser to the government. At first Sir Ernest declined, due to the contemptible calumnies in the press. Yet in the end he was persuaded to accompany an Anglo-French mission to negotiate a war loan in the United States. Largely through his Wall Street contacts, a loan was raised for 500 million dollars. Incredibly, on learning of Cassel's successful transactions, the Anti-German League attempted in the High Court to show cause why he should now 'be removed from his membership of the Privy Council and have his British naturalization rescinded'. The litigation dragged on for some months until the petition was finally dismissed.

Edwina, who experienced an unhappy childhood, was nine years old when her mother died. Wilfred Ashley, who was created Lord Mount Temple, shackled himself to parliamentary duties, and apparently spent little time with his daughters. (Edwina's sister Mary was born in 1904.) When, in the summer of 1914, he told Edwina in his study at Broadlands, his Hampshire estate, that he was going to marry again – this time to divorcée Mrs Mary (Molly) Forbes-Sempell – she was deeply resentful. The dislike between Edwina and her stepmother was mutual. Not surprisingly, therefore, Edwina was sent to a boarding school at Eastbourne, which she detested, and then to the first domestic science college in England. With the specific object of learning to be competent housewives, the students did all the work, including the cooking and scrubbing of floors. Whatever motive had lurked in the mind of the second Mrs Ashley in sending her stepdaughter there, Edwina's training would be invaluable in the Second World War.

Instead of going to a finishing school, Edwina was permitted to visit Italy. On her return to Broadlands, however, the question arose as to her future, until Sir Ernest Cassel asked the Ashleys to allow his young and attractive grand-daughter, now brooding under the dominance of her stepmother, to be his hostess at Brook House. She was seventeen then, and the guests – among them the most eminent personalities of the day – were invariably two generations older than the slim, self-willed girl. Entertaining on this grandiose scale was costly, but, one writer claims, Edwina's personal allowance from her grandfather was rather modest.

Towards the end of his life a change came over Sir Ernest. It is said that hitherto he had rarely, if at all, inquired into the welfare of his staff. Now he was more solicitous. Once he remarked to his secretary, Miss Stella Underhill: 'I think you must have had a very much happier home than I had when I was young.'

During August 1921 he purchased for £88,000, at Cap Ferrat, the exquisite Villa des Cèdres, previously the favourite residence of King Leopold of the Belgians and his morganatic wife. But Sir Ernest never resided there. Almost exactly a month later – on 21 September – he died. At seven o'clock in the evening, while delivering a telegram, a footman found Sir Ernest alone, collapsed over his desk in his opulent study. His heart had failed him.

Edwina had been staying at a house-party at Dunrobin Castle, the home of the Duke and Duchess of Sutherland. Another guest, Lieutenant Lord Louis Mountbatten, had already left to attend his father's funeral and had planned to meet Edwina in London, by coincidence on the day that her grandfather died. Sir Ernest and Prince Louis died within eleven days of each other, neither having the remotest idea that their respective grand-daughter and son would soon enter into the most glamorous marriage in Britain.

In the meantime, a surprise awaited Sir Ernest's acquaintances and closest intimates: the announcement of his requiem mass at the Catholic Church of the Immaculate Conception in Farm Street, Mayfair. The story of his conversion after the death of his wife had remained a guarded secret. The courtiers and politicians, the moguls from the great finance houses in the City of London, and others who gazed on the silver coffin containing the mortal remains of the Jew from Cologne, were astonished to discover his adherence to the Catholic faith.

9

A Unique Achievement

It is reputed that Sir Ernest's net estate totalled some six million pounds and that Edwina was the main beneficiary. She was still entitled, however, to nothing more than a modest allowance until she married or attained the age of twenty-one.

Edwina Ashley waved farewell to Lord Louis, then embarking in the *Renown* with the Prince of Wales, on 26 October 1921. Her impoverished state did not lessen her determination to visit him in India. The £100 advanced by her aunt only catered for a second-class fare, but the Socialist-minded Edwina was not deterred by this; nor did the problems that harassed her until she finally reached Delhi. During the six days they were together, Lord Louis proposed at Viceregal Lodge and was promptly accepted.

The royal tour of India captured much of the imperial pomp of some half-century earlier. The bejewelled reigning princes and the swarming crowds were there. Yet a shadow was darkening the Indian scene – that of Mahatma Gandhi. Lord Louis would have to cope with his fanatical followers when eventually he presided over Britain's imperial demise. Many ignored the boycotting of the tour which Gandhi demanded, but extremists – equally disregarding his command to restrict their actions to peaceful resistance – tried forcibly to dispel the crowds on the royal entourage's first day in Bombay. Only in sacred Benares, and in Allahabad, where Pandit Nehru was incarcerated in a British gaol, was the boycott abundantly clear; the Prince and Lord Louis passed along empty streets between shuttered houses.

When the *Renown* returned to Britain on 20 June 1922, Lord Louis discovered that Edwina, with characteristic bustle, had already initiated the wedding plans. At first Princess Victoria expressed doubts about the suitability of the match. Edwina was an heiress of incredible affluence; Louis, despite his ancient pedigree, was a young naval officer of modest means. But she wrote to Edwina that she had made Dickie happy by accepting him –

for he loves you dearly & that you should love him too brings you near to my heart ... It is not always easy being the wife of a naval man & the many separations hit one hard. Yet I & Dickie's father were very happy in spite of them & I hope you will be able to take much pride & interest in his career for that helps a lot, & to my mind a man without a profession leads a poor sort of life & when one cares for a man, one does not want him to be a slacker or stand in the way of his work, or make him feel that one grudges him the place it must take in his life and feelings . . .

The wedding, at St Margaret's, Westminster, on 18 July 1922, had all the charisma of a royal event. King George v and Queen Mary gave it the royal seal of approval by attending, as did many European grand dukes and grand duchesses, princes and princesses, and an impressive cross-section of the British aristocracy. The Prince of Wales was Louis's best man.

If Princess Victoria believed that her son, married to someone so rich, might lose the incentive to seek advancement on merit in the navy, she had not reckoned on her son's dedication to vindicate the unwarranted disgrace of his father. After six months' honeymoon on half pay touring the Continent and America, Lord Louis earnestly resumed his naval career. The Mountbattens' reputation as hedonists also belied the seriousness with which Louis approached his naval duties.

For two years he served with the battleship *Revenge*. Again, there arose a parallel between his career and that of his father: he joined his ship in Constantinople, where the Mediterranean Fleet was guarding the Dardanelles against a resurgent Turkish army which had cast out the Greeks in Smyrna. In 1924 Lord Louis began a Long Signals Course at Portsmouth, living with his wife and their first daughter, Patricia at Adsdean, a large country house not far from the base. The social life was intensive but did not impede Louis from passing out first in his class. During April, two years later, his appointment as flag lieutenant to Vice-Admiral Sir Rudolf Bentinck, then commanding the Reserve Fleet and flying his flag in the *Centurion*, was merely the prelude to his selection as assistant fleet wireless officer to the commander-in-chief, Mediterranean, Admiral Sir Roger Keyes. To the annoyance of critics, Lord Louis would succeed the Admiral as Chief of Combined Operations in the Second World War.

During July 1928, Lord Louis was appointed flotilla signal officer of the Second Destroyer Flotilla in the *Stuart*, the year Lady Mountbatten gave birth to their second daughter, Pamela. The flotilla had called at Barcelona and Lord Louis had gone ashore to meet his wife at the Ritz Hotel, when she suddenly informed him that the baby was about to arrive. One would have thought that the hotel manager could have recommended an appropriate doctor, but he could not. In desperation Louis telephoned his cousin, Queen Ena, in Madrid, but she was not available. Even King Alfonso was unhelpful; he knew of no doctor in Barcelona but offered to send a military guard to the hotel. Finally, Louis was forced to rely on the services of a throat specialist who was aided by a nun. King Alfonso agreed to be the child's godfather.

After a brief period of home service, Lord Louis returned to the Mediterranean as fleet wireless officer in the *Queen Elizabeth*. Clearly he had inherited his father's skills. Prince Louis had been noted as a signals expert; so, too, was his son, and of such brilliant attainments that he held displays of fleet communication in a special centre in Malta;

the Admiralty and various vessels of the fleet combined. Prince Louis had invented the course indicator; Lord Louis devised the station-keeper, which measured the correct distance of a ship from the one ahead. Both devices are used by the Royal Navy to this day.

Lord Louis was twenty-seven when he was promoted to lieutenant-commander. One reason for this early promotion was that he had seen service at sea about a year and a half before the normal age, and due to the seniority acquired in his sub-lieutenant's examination. Five years later he gained the rank of commander. His first command was the destroyer *Daring* which, steaming to Singapore, he exchanged for the *Wishart*, a much older destroyer. Despite her age, her crew (as in the case of his father's earliest commands) gained most of the trophies in the annual Mediterranean regatta. Mountbatten infused his crews with his forceful personality and enthusiasm – qualities which perhaps accounted for his appointment to Whitehall in 1936 for duties with the Director of the Naval Air Division.

Controversy had broken out between the Admiralty and the Air Ministry over the dual control of the Fleet Air Arm. In the current arrangement, the navy manned and controlled the carriers, and the Royal Air Force supervised the fighting personnel. To be the liaison in negotiations between both ministries and ministers, politicians and senior officers, was a role that appealed to Lord Louis and, by a coincidence, was redolent of the time his father had acted in a similar capacity during friction between the navy and the army over naval armament control. Finally, the Fleet Air Arm was allotted to the Admiralty, but not coastal reconnaissance or convoy protection.

Louis's charm, foresight and persistency – and his zest for a good idea – won for Britain an invention which, spurned at first by the United States Ordnance Department, had at first met with similar scepticism among Britain's naval hierarchy.

During 1937, Lord Louis was introduced to Mr Anton Gazda, an Austrian engineer, who, fleeing to Switzerland from Nazi aggression, obtained the rights of a quick-firing gun built at the Oerlikon works in Zurich. Re-designing it to fire five hundred shells a minute (a figure which was later exceeded), Gazda realized that this was the counter to the Luftwaffe's dive-bombers. Time would confirm the accuracy of this belief, but, with the exception of Lord Louis, he met with a lukewarm reception in Britain. Before Gazda left for Switzerland, Lord Mountbatten extracted a promise that he would withhold the gun from other nations until the Admiralty finally decided. It is claimed that the totalitarian states and Japan were keen to buy it. Indeed, Prince Chichibu, the Japanese Emperor's brother, is believed to have tempted Gazda with £400,000 as well as royalties.

Another two years elapsed, a period embracing many demonstrations and talks, before the Admiralty accepted the gun. The Oerlikon device, the most effective weapon against aerial attack, was mounted on British warships in September and October 1939, among them Louis's next command – the destroyer *Kelly*. By then, he had been promoted to captain, some days before his thirty-seventh birthday. As experienced by Prince Louis of Battenberg, advancement to senior rank – in the son's case several years before the accepted norm – triggered off insinuations of favouritism. Wild innuendo, however, is no substitute for fact. Whereas social connections might ease the way to promotion in junior appointments, only merit can be the deciding factor in promotion to a senior rank.

Lord Louis realized the ambition that escaped his father – the exciting experience of commanding a warship in action. The father had gained distinction with a cruiser squadron; the son would enhance his reputation in destroyers. For two years after the outbreak of war, Lord Louis commanded a destroyer flotilla and achieved enduring fame in one particular vessel – the *Kelly*. His ship would be savagely battered three times; only in the last action would he fail to bring the *Kelly* back to port.

A few days before the holocaust began, Lord Louis told the 240 members of his crew:

In peace time it takes all of three weeks to get a new ship's company together, to let them sling their hammocks and teach them their stations and various duties, to get all the cordite and shells and oil fuel and stores on board, and so on and so forth. Well, you've read your papers and you know that Ribbentrop signed a non-aggression pact with Stalin yesterday. As I see it, that means war next week. So I will give you not three weeks but three days to get this ship ready to sail.

None of us will take off our clothes or sling our hammocks, or turn in for the next three days and nights, until the job is finished. Then we'll send Hitler a signal saying 'The *Kelly*'s ready – you can start your war.'

For Princess Victoria, hostilities had inbuilt tragedies. As in the First World War, close relations were in conflict. Her sons George and Louis, her grandsons Philip and David, and her German grandsons-in-law would fight on opposing sides. To Lord Louis she wrote: 'You have so much of Papa's nature in you, so much of his sensitiveness, so that I through this trait of his know how much you suffer, & perhaps it is well for you as he used to say of himself, that a certain hardness in one's wife is a help against this sensitiveness torturing one uselessly.'

Lord Louis shared his mother's fondness for poetry, and at his request she sent him poems which he took to sea. In the accompanying letter, she revealed: 'It is strange, comparing this war with the last, how terribly matter-of-fact this age is. Not one paper I have seen has a poem that has moved me, & they contain very few.'

The Second World War dispelled the frivolous image with which the public had for so long identified Lord Louis. The emergency, and the tasks he would be called upon to fulfil, even in the earliest months of hostilities, revealed his true stature. He was seen as a tactician and an undaunted, enterprising commander. Though a strict disciplinarian, his treatment of his crews was leavened with magnanimity and justice. While his flotilla was patrolling the convoy lanes in home waters, the *Kelly* struck a mine in December 1939. Terrified, a stoker deserted his post and dashed on deck, prepared to abandon ship. For the moment, Lord Mountbatten's primary concern was to get his damaged vessel back to harbour, which he accomplished, then he placed the man under arrest. To general surprise, some hours later he called the ship's company together and said:

Out of 240 men on board this ship, 239 behaved as they ought to have ... but one was unable to control himself and deserted his post, and incidentally his comrades in the engine-room. I had him brought before me a couple of hours ago, and he himself informed me that he knew that the punishment for desertion of his post could be death. You will therefore be surprised to hear that I propose to let him off with a 'caution'. One caution to him, and a second one to myself, for having failed in four months to impress my personality and doctrine on each and all of you to prevent such incidents from occurring.

From now on I wish to make it clear I expect everyone to behave in the way the 239 did, and to stick to their post in action to the last. I will under no circumstances whatever again tolerate the slightest suspicion of cowardice or indiscipline, and I know that from now on none of you will present me with such a problem.

Repaired at Hebburn-on-Tyne, where she was built, the redoubtable *Kelly* proceeded to Scapa Flow for further patrolling, there colliding with the destroyer *Ghurka* – who was off course – in a snowstorm. This time she was made seaworthy in the London Graving Dock before helping to evacuate British troops from Namsos in Norway. Commanding a flotilla of four British destroyers and the French destroyer *Bison*, Lord Louis's duties were to screen the fleet of Rear-Admiral John Cunningham.

Leaving Scapa Flow on 29 April 1940, the ships assembled at Kya Light, some seventy miles south of Namsos. Fog impeded the progress of the cruiser *York* and three transports, but Lord Louis, using the murk to protect his ship from aerial attack, scouted ahead with the destroyers. In a sense the decision was foolhardy, for the flotilla almost ran into a rocky promontory.

When visibility improved on the afternoon of 1 May, Cunningham ordered the attempt to reach their objective. Lord Louis led along Nansenfjord, a deep and somewhat narrow channel allowing little scope for manoeuvre if the Luftwaffe struck. Curiously, German aircraft were notably absent, enabling the fleet to pass into the broad harbour where Namsos burned. Houses, warehouses and great supplies of stores were engulfed in flames, against which five thousand troops waited anxiously for rescue. Beginning at 10.30 at night, the evacuation was completed at 2.20 the next morning. By incredible luck the enemy had not intervened. But good fortune ended shortly after dawn. First came the reconnaissance planes, then for hours the air was rent with the screams of bombers. The *Bison* was reduced to a fiery wreck, and the *Afridi*, trying to rescue survivors, turned turtle and sank after two direct hits. Other than that, the rest of the fleet escaped unscathed.

The *Kelly*'s crew received little respite. After joining the cruiser *Birmingham* at nightfall on 9 May, Lord Louis and his flotilla searched for a German mine-layer and E-boats, operating, it was reported, off the coast of Holland. Mist was forming, making visibility poor, when a look-out, noticing a seething wake, shouted: 'Torpedo!' There was no scope for evasive action. As the torpedo crashed on the port side amidships, a flame shot higher than the bridge. A great gash, many yards long, had been torn in the *Kelly*'s side; she lay motionless, with a pronounced list, and rail awash. Lord Louis ordered the torpedoes and depth charges to be jettisoned, but getting a line to the *Bulldog* was less simple; it was about 11 pm before the stricken ship was taken in tow. Only the emergency tiller aft could be used for steering, and a row of men relayed instructions from the bridge to the crew who worked it.

Soon after midnight a German E-boat burst out of the darkness. Striking the *Bulldog* a glancing blow, it careered along the tow-rope, crashing on to the listing *Kelly*, then blew up as it slid off the stern.

For four days German bombers strove madly to deliver the *coup de grâce* as the *Bulldog* hauled the tangled hulk. Sometimes Lord Louis himself operated one of the guns. To make matters worse, the rope sometimes broke, leaving the *Kelly* in a dangerous plight. On the third night Lord Louis and his skeleton crew abandoned ship, but when she stayed afloat they boarded her again the next morning. In one of the war's epic feats, Lord Louis brought his ship back to Britain, taking the useless hulk up river to Hebburn-on-Tyne.

For his stubbornness and bravery, Lord Louis was awarded the Distinguished Service Order. Conscious of the jealousy her son sometimes evoked, Princess Victoria observed: 'On the whole, it is a good thing he did not get it till after everybody had heard or read the details ... Now no one can in fairness say that he has not fully earned it.'

Lord Louis's heroic act, which raised morale in Britain, was not achieved without fear. Years later, addressing the Military Academy at Dehra Dun, when he was Governor-General of India, he recounted his action in that incident:

... after my flotilla leader, the *Kelly*, had been torpedoed off a German minefield in the North Sea, an enemy E-boat came out of the darkness and opened fire, as it shot past us, at the bridge on which I was standing, with a 20-mm pom-pom. This was at 20–30 yards' range. I was alone on the bridge as my damaged ship was being towed back, and the survivors were busy trying to prevent the ship from turning over. I ducked down behind the bridge screen, a very silly thing to do, for it would not have kept out a rifle bullet. Then I suddenly felt frightfully ashamed and very glad I was alone on the bridge so that no one had seen me duck. I said to myself: 'Never again will I permit myself to show when I am afraid.'

While the *Kelly* was undergoing repairs, Lord Louis took command of the *Javelin*. He continued:

Next time I was in a different destroyer of my flotilla, the *Javelin*, when we met an enemy destroyer flotilla in the Channel. It was a pitch black night in the days before radar had got going, so we almost ran into each other before we opened fire. We fired a split second before the Germans. Photographs taken were subsequently measured and showed that the range on opening fire between the two leading destroyers was 900 yards. The enemy destroyer fired a broadside with her five 5·1-inch guns. As you are soldiers and not sailors, I will compare this with a land situation. It was exactly as though you were standing on an exposed target – 900 yards from a medium battery opening fire across open sights. I don't mind admitting it put the wind up me, so I regret to say I stepped off the compass platform for a moment. Then I quickly glanced at a convenient instrument; I looked to see if it was all right, and then stepped back on to the compass platform. I got away with it because people did not realize why I stepped down ...

After that action Lord Mountbatten was criticized, accused of displaying reckless-ness, deploying his ships in the wrong formation and delaying to open fire for three critical minutes; briefly, he had allowed the enemy to escape. The fact is that two tor-pedoes hit the *Javelin* fore and aft. Both bows and stern were shattered completely. Con-fusion prevailed as to which ship had been struck. Hence the delay before the next senior captain took command. Indeed, it was much to Lord Louis's annoyance that the enemy disappeared behind an effective smoke-screen.

He commanded his squadron from various ships before the *Kelly* returned to opera-tional duties. Her commission to the Mediterranean during the frightful days in Crete would be her last. She turned turtle at thirty knots after a Stuka's bomb crashed through the deck and blew away much of her keel. Many of the crew died with her. With other survivors, Lord Louis was rescued by the *Kipling* and conveyed to Alexandria. 'There may be less than half of the *Kelly* [crew] left,' he said, taking leave of his men, 'but I feel each of us will take up the battle with even stronger heart . . . You will all be sent to replace men who have been killed in other ships, and the next time you are in action, remember the *Kelly*. As you ram each shell home into the gun, shout "Kelly!" and so her spirit will go on inspiring us until victory is won.'

Returning to Britain, Lord Louis was assigned the command of the aircraft carrier *Illustrious* which, badly mauled in the Mediterranean, was being repaired under Lend-Lease in the Norfolk Navy Yard in the United States. He travelled to America, but other plans were materializing; indeed, the *Kelly* would be his last wartime sea-going command. A puzzled Lord Louis was summoned hurriedly to London to a meeting with Churchill; the war-leader had telegraphed on 10 October 1941 explaining that he was needed 'for something which you will find of the highest interest'. At forty-one, soaring over senior contemporaries and succeeding the testy Admiral of the Fleet Sir Roger Keyes, the hero of Zeebrugge, Mountbatten was suddenly elevated to become adviser to Combined Operations Command. Once again, promotion gave rise to jealousy and tremors of indignation. Just as Horatio Bottomley, in his magazine *John Bull*, had criticized Lord Louis's father during the First World War, so now Lord Beaverbrook and the *Daily Express* directed a vitriolic attack against Lord Louis himself. It revived wounding recollections for Princess Victoria, who now assured her son: 'Luckily the general public is not much perturbed by the *Daily Express*'s outcries & scandal-sniffing.'

To what extent, if at all, Churchill was compensating the son for the harsh treatment of a wronged father, one cannot say. Maybe Lord Louis's dynamism and readiness to innovate influenced Churchill's choice. In any event, Lord Louis never gave Churchill cause to regret the appointment. Churchill briefed him that his cardinal object would be 'the invasion of Europe, for unless we return to the Continent and beat the Germans on land we shall never win the war. All the other headquarters in this country are thinking defensively. Your job is to be offensive; train for the offensive; work out the craft, the equipment, the tactics, the administration and everything needed to sustain the offensive ... The south of England is now a bastion against German invasion; you will turn it into the springboard from which to launch our invasion.'

At the outset, Lord Louis received the rank of acting commodore. On the surface, this was down-grading – purely out of deference to the chiefs of staff – for Keyes had been Director of Combined Operations. In due course, however, he was promoted to Chief of Combined Operations with the ranks of vice-admiral, lieutenant-general and air marshal, a distinction without precedent. Furthermore, he now attended meetings of the chiefs of staff. But again the rumblings of controversy grew loud. Some vociferous members of the service clubs raged against the promotion, treating it as a personal insult, but Churchill claimed that Lord Louis's exploits and abilities fitted him ideally for the post.

Temperamentally, Mountbatten was an admirable choice, for he was unfettered by inflexible military dogma and was not hidebound by orthodoxy. Moreover, there was his enthusiasm – almost fetish – for invention. The heterogeneous body of men with whom he had to deal comprised scientists, a hotch-potch of men from the universities and industry, officers of unconventional turn of mind, and men from the three services notorious for their toughness.

No inventor was discouraged from displaying what might be a potential weapon of war. Many ideas were discarded, but others were of paramount value: among them the amphibious tank and the portable Mulberry floating harbours used in the Normandy landing. The Germans never anticipated the latter; quite wrongly, they had reckoned that no invasion could succeed without enemy access to one of the larger ports. Of similar strategic value were the Pluto pipelines which carried oil beneath the English Channel from Britain to France. To Lord Louis's own credit were the floating head-quarters for mammoth amphibious operations, from which a commander-in-chief could communicate with his forces on sea and land and in the air. For this he drew on his technical skills and wealth of knowledge of wireless communication.

To most people, Combined Operations signified audacious raids on Vaagsö, Bruneval, St Nazaire, Dieppe and other strategic points along the fringe of Nazi-occupied Europe. These attacks were generally hailed to be on vital targets and nothing more. But the aim was more momentous, especially as regards Dieppe. Assault tech-niques had to be tested to assess any weaknesses before the mass invasion of Normandy could be attempted. The attack on Dieppe, with its appreciable loss of life, was to many an abject failure. But data of paramount value was gleaned to ensure greater success in future operations.

During his two years with Combined Operations, Lord Louis accumulated the requisite knowledge for the astute planning of amphibious operations in North Africa and Sicily. The essence of such planning would be the landing of Allied forces along the Second Front.

The final phase was the most critical of Lord Louis's wartime career. Frustrations and the acute problems encountered might have resulted in dismal failure; instead he emerged from the hostilities as one of the great architects of victory.

Churchill was dissatisfied with the stagnation and military chaos in Burma. The Japanese had over-run South-East Asia as far as the India–Burma border, and were even menacing India itself. Thus Churchill proposed a new independent South-East Asia Command with Mountbatten as Supreme Allied Commander. Broaching the matter at a meeting of Anglo-American Chiefs of Staff at the Quebec Conference, agreement was unanimous. But the appointment again provoked comment. Informed by Churchill of his proposal during the voyage to Canada, Sir Alan Brooke, Chief of the Imperial General Staff, wrote later: 'This was the first time I had heard of Mountbatten's suggested appointment ... He had never commanded more than destroyers ... what he lacked in experience he made up in self-confidence. He had boundless energy and drive.' When Lord Louis subsequently sought Brooke's advice, Sir Alan advised: 'It is a maritime thing out there, amphibious stuff. I think you should do it.'

On his arrival at Delhi, Mountbatten learned that his 14th Army had 126 casualties due to disease for every man wounded. Morale was alarmingly low and supplies were in a deplorable state – an unenviable inheritance. The Admiralty interfered with his naval units, and American bomber and transport crews took their instructions from Washington. The Supremo had also to cope with the inexorable demands of Generalissimo Chiang Kai-Shek for arms and material for his dual conflict with the Japanese and Chinese Communists. Irksome, too, was the exasperating personality of his deputy, General Stillwell, commonly known as 'Vinegar Joe', who failed to grasp the purpose of Lord Louis's strategy.

Mountbatten personally visited the units of his 'forgotten' forces, injecting them with his unmistakable brand of confidence. He arranged for them to have their own newspaper, ensured that supplies were no longer haphazard and reinvigorated hospital and transport facilities and leave centres. Above all, he exploded the myth among troops and Asians of Japanese invincibility. His surprise tactics, compelling the enemy to fight throughout the five months of shocking monsoon rains, reaped magnificent dividends. Ruthlessly engaging the enemy in jungle and disease-infested swamp, the 14th Army had regained Burma by May 1945.

Plans for the conquest of Malaya – a massive assault christened 'Operation Zipper'

– never matured; Japanese aggression ended dramatically after the radio-active clouds rose over Nagasaki and Hiroshima.

For Lord Louis at his headquarters at Kandy in Ceylon, peace harvested its problems and widespread chaos. His salient priority was to safeguard and repatriate Allied prisoners-of-war and civilian internees, duties in which he was fortified by his wife, who organized rest centres, hospitals and the allocation of food. The neutralizing of fanatical enemy troops was also urgent. Perhaps more stupendous than anything was the task of administering an area the size of Europe in which millions of Asians, many of whom were suffering from varying degrees of starvation, were fermenting political unrest. Nationalism was rampant. Lord Louis was averse to enforcing a return to pre-war colonialism; national resurgence was now too potent to ignore. It was his liberalism which stirred up reactionary fury and obstruction in the former Dutch and French colonies of Indonesia and Indo-China.

Mountbatten found himself increasingly enmeshed in politics, a situation which led to his first meeting with Pandit Nehru. With other Indian Congress leaders, Nehru had been released from gaol and now proposed to visit Indian communities in Malaya. When he announced his intention of meeting members of the former anti-British Indian National Army (which had been created by the Japanese) in Singapore, the British military authorities, fearing outbreaks of violence, decided on the extensive use of security troops. A livid Mountbatten, instructing officialdom to extend courtesy to Nehru, entertained the Indian leader at Government House and arranged for Indians living in remoter areas to visit him. Surprised by this unexpected civility, Nehru deliberately omitted to pay tribute to the disbanded Indian National Army.

When his duties as Supremo were concluded in June 1946, Lord Louis wished to renew his naval career. Thus the youngest Supreme Allied Commander of the Second World War expected to attend a senior officers' staff course as a prelude to commanding the First Cruiser Squadron in the Mediterranean in the following year. But his talents were to be employed elsewhere. Maybe it was Lord Louis's firm rejection of colonialism in South-East Asia which influenced Clement Attlee. At least in December 1946 the Labour Prime Minister approached Louis, now Earl Mountbatten of Burma, with a proposal that would test his adroitness in conducting negotiations: the ending of the British Raj on the Indian sub-continent.

Sir Stafford Cripps's mission to arrange self-government had been wrecked by the rancour between Hindus and Muslims. Friction erupted in bloody clashes, and Field Marshal Lord Wavell, then Viceroy, advocated a systematic withdrawal of the British civil service and armed forces. To Attlee this was a betrayal of responsibility. Then he had 'an inspiration', as he later explained. 'I thought of Mountbatten. He had an extremely lively, exciting personality. He had an extraordinary faculty for getting on with all kinds of people . . . He was also blessed with a very unusual wife. So I put it to him. Bit of a shock for him, because one of Dickie's greatest hopes was that

Lady Louis Mountbatten and her daughters (Patricia and Pamela), father (Colonel Wilfred Ashley, later Lord Mount Temple) and Douglas Fairbanks, the Hollywood film actor.

Lord Mountbatten emerged from the Second World War as one of the great architects of victory. Here he is pictured with a fighter pilot in Burma, where he had been appointed Supreme Allied Commander.

he would one day succeed to the position of First Sea Lord from which his father had been most disgracefully thrown out in the anti-German cry at the beginning of the First World War ...'

At first Earl Mountbatten wavered, shrinking from the office of Viceroy, until King George VI backed Attlee's plan. Princess Victoria, however, suspicious of politicians' intentions, took a less sanguine attitude. They had ruined her husband; she had no desire to see them destroy her son. She feared that, apart from hindering his naval career, Lord Louis would be used as the scapegoat for the politicians' shortcomings. 'Politicians are incorrigible!' she warned him.

Earl Mountbatten reached Delhi on 22 March 1947, with the brief to liquidate British rule and ensure political independence and self-determination for 450 million people. 'We are a great nation,' he announced, 'but we can no longer rule you ... I shall need the greatest goodwill of the greatest possible number, and I am asking India today for that goodwill.'

The majority of the Indian leaders, such as Gandhi, Jinnah and Nehru, extended that goodwill. Where it was not forthcoming, Mountbatten applied pressure to effect a compromise. It was reckoned that speed in transferring power was imperative if smouldering communal antagonisms were not to burst into a conflagration of disorder and even massacre. Previously the date for setting up self-government in the new states of India and Pakistan had been arranged for June 1948. But Earl Mountbatten persuaded the British Government and Hindu and Muslim leaders to agree to 14 August 1947. As midnight approached on Independence Day, Pandit Nehru said to the Constituent Assembly: '... At the stroke of the midnight hour, when the world sleeps, India will wake to life and freedom.' It would wake to much more. Meanwhile, on the following day Earl Mountbatten agreed, at the request of the Indian Assembly, to be the first Governor-General.

Although the British Government supplied the blueprint by which power was transferred, it was Mountbatten's task to define it to the sub-continent's teeming millions. Attlee had maintained that 'the odds were six to four against success'. With such marked divergences in caste and religion, errors and pitfalls were inescapable. The Tories, even Mountbatten's friend Winston Churchill, accused him of identifying himself with a policy of 'scuttle'. The Muslims condemned him for what they alleged was bias in favour of the Hindus. Many censured him because he failed – so they contended – to anticipate the blood-letting and even large-scale killing. Not long after partition, millions of Hindus, Muslims and Sikhs crossed the new frontier in migratory hordes, culminating in a turmoil of homeless refugees. The death toll mounted amid the hysteria of religious hatred and communal rioting. It can be argued that, in the circumstances, perhaps this was inevitable; that the horrors would have been of greater magnitude if the transfer of power had been delayed. It is equally significant that no British politician placed himself in such a precarious situation as Earl Mountbatten.

He quit India in June 1948. By now an earl and a Privy Councillor, and accepted

Lady Brabourne (Patricia Mountbatten) with her mother at a party given to naval personnel and their families in Malta.

Earl Mountbatten of Burma, seen here in the robes of the Order of the Bath, imprinted his ideas on Britain's defence organization during a decade in Whitehall.

into the Order of the Garter, he was gazetted rear-admiral and commanded the First Cruiser Squadron in Malta. The next year he was promoted to vice-admiral and during 1950 he rose to Fourth Sea Lord, in charge of the navy's administrative planning. Promotion was rapid. From commander-in-chief, Mediterranean Fleet, he graduated to commander-in-chief, Allied Forces Mediterranean, co-ordinating strategical planning and communications between the Middle East and Supreme Allied Headquarters and NATO in Europe.

In 1955 he achieved the ambition for which he had striven since adolescence. Forty-one years after his father had been shamefully ousted as professional head of the navy, Earl Mountbatten attained the dignity of First Sea Lord. He took the Royal Navy into the age of the carrier task-force, guided-missile ships and nuclear submarines, and in 1959, then Chief of the Defence Staff and Chairman of the Chiefs of Staff Committee, he instigated – much to the resentment of the traditionalists – the scheme for unified defence. The cynics scoffed that 'Dickie does everything for an audience of one', yet, whether his ideas were correct or not, he imprinted them on Britain's defence organization during a decade in Whitehall.

To Earl Mountbatten the year of his retirement from naval affairs, 1965, was notable for a great personal loss: the death of his sister Louise. As a family, the Mountbattens were devoted to each other. Like their mother, Louis and Louise were inclined to talk openly. Earl Mountbatten has since explained that he and his sister

babbled endlessly . . . Louise and I were extremely close to one another, both when we were young and in later life. This may have been because her elder sister Alice married in 1903, our brother George in 1916, and she and I were married within a year of each other in 1923 and 1922 respectively, so we were the ones who were always at home together. But it was more than this, we thought the same, we spoke alike, we were deeply devoted to each other and we constantly corresponded with each other. And later, when we were married, we often visited each other, either I and my wife going to Sweden or she and her husband coming to Malta or England.

Princess Louise of Battenberg (later known as Lady Louise Mountbatten) was born on 13 July 1889 at Heiligenberg, where Princess Victoria was staying with her mother-in-law while Prince Louis served in the Mediterranean Fleet. According to Princess Victoria, Louise was 'rather a miserable little object' so that Prince Louis nicknamed her 'Shrimp' – a soubriquet that endured throughout a happy childhood. Life was nomadic, including visits to Queen Victoria at Osborne, where to each child the matriarch gave a shilling for the collection at Sunday services. 'But it was with some hesitation that I put the shilling in,' Louise later told a friend. 'For, as children, we were brought up with very little money of our own.'

The Battenbergs spent a fair amount of time at Court. During 1909, for instance, Prince Louis and his family stayed at Windsor for the visit of King Manoel of Portugal who, later that year, proposed marriage to Louise. King Edward VII, ever keen to see members of the British royal family occupying foreign thrones, favoured the match. But he was resisted; again, Battenberg will-power was pre-eminent; Louise was not in love with Manoel and declined. Her action was fortunate; in the following year revolution forced the Braganzas into exile.

In those days, to Louise the prospect of queenship was quite unnerving, yet circumstances would change her mind after the First World War. By then her mind would be scarred by the outrage on her father, but the resentment that Prince Louis's resignation generated in her brother did not deter her from answering the country's call. At first she worked with the Soldiers and Sailors Families' Association and then an organization called 'Smokes for Soldiers and Sailors'. This, however, failed to satisfy the Battenberg spirit for action and even danger. Louise therefore trained as a nurse for the Voluntary Aid Detachments and was attached to an improvised military hospital at Nevers in France. In 1917 – the year her title was reduced to that of Lady Louise Mountbatten – she moved to the Princess Club Hospital in Bermondsey and two years later worked for three months in a French hospital for bone tuberculosis at Palaves near Montpellier. For her nursing services, Louise was awarded the War Medal of Great Britain 1914–18, the British Red Cross Medal, the *Medaille de la Reconnaissance Française* and the Italian Red Cross Medal.

The first World War and its aftermath was probably the most exacting, even agonizing, period for Louise and her family. As well as the distressing affair at the Admiralty, they were haunted by anxiety about the fate of relatives abroad. The Russian Revolution had callously destroyed the imperial family. Some of the Battenbergs' German relations had lost their thrones, among them Princess Victoria's brother, the Grand Duke Ernest Louis of Hesse-Darmstadt. Her sister, Princess Irene of Prussia, had been compelled to flee from the naval mutineers at Kiel, and in Greece political instability had resulted in the assassination of King George I and the exile of the royal family, including Princess Alice, her sister. Living with Prince Louis and Princess Victoria, Louise witnessed the unhappiness that tragedy created for her parents.

Early in 1922, after the death of Prince Louis, Louise shared apartments with her mother at Kensington Palace. But her stay there was relatively short. In November the next year she married Crown Prince Gustav Adolf of Sweden at the Chapel Royal in St James's Palace. Earlier, news of the betrothal had sparked off concern in Sweden; a worried government queried whether Lady Louise was of royal blood since the heir to the Swedish throne was debarred from the succession if he married a commoner. Stanley Baldwin, the Prime Minister, allayed the anxiety of his Swedish counterpart by sending him an official printed list of precedence at Court.

As a Mountbatten, it would have been out of character if Crown Princess Louise had not left some impact on the country of her adoption. She openly extolled the Swedish notion of democracy and encouraged it. 'The foundations of this attitude', Earl Mountbatten has revealed, 'had been laid during her childhood. For we were brought up in freedom of thought and freedom of opinion, in keeping with our own times. Our mother, who was a remarkable woman, had far-sighted ideas in many fields.'

One can therefore sense Crown Princess Louise's abhorrence of Nazism in the Second World War. Sadly, relatives again found themselves on opposing sides, but because of Swedish neutrality, Louise was able to serve as a go-between, relaying domestic information – even though it was somewhat spasmodic – between relatives in Germany, Britain, Greece and elsewhere. In gratitude, they presented her with a gold case designed like an envelope, engraved with all their names, on her seventieth birthday.

On 29 October 1950 Gustav, the old King of Sweden, died peacefully at Drottningholm in his ninety-third year. King Gustav VI and Queen Louise succeeded to the throne, making many changes at Court: where possible they discouraged formality. Queen Louise was a human dynamo in palace affairs, helping to bind the royal family close to the people. As a woman from Dalarna in central Sweden remarked after a visit of the King and Queen: 'We found her a personality with style and will and a good person with enough imagination to be able to put herself in other people's situations and therefore to understand them. She did not just show herself and utter the usual conventional phrases, but she really identified herself with each and everyone's daily life.'

But the dynamo ceased to hum. While Princess Alice of Greece, who had promised to celebrate her eightieth birthday in Stockholm, was visiting, Queen Louise was taken to hospital in great pain, doctors disclosing that she had a blood clot in the lower part of the main artery leading to her heart. She survived the operation but died three days later – on 7 March 1965. Among the numerous wreaths at the funeral at Stockholm's most ancient shrine, the Great Church in the Old City, on an island in the North Channel, was one composed of irises and red amaryllis. One of the ribbons, which were in the British colours, bore the name 'Dickie'; the other, inscribed in gold lettering, contained the words: 'In very loving memory of my darling sister Louise.'

10

The Greek Connection

LIKE Queen Ena of Spain and the Tsarina Alicky of Russia, when Princess Alice of Battenberg – the future mother of Prince Philip – agreed to marry, she exposed herself to the chicaneries of politics.

After four centuries of servitude under the Ottoman Turks, in the 1820s the Greeks, intoxicated by their hard-won liberty, had looked towards the Protecting Powers (Britain, Russia and France) for a king. Prince Leopold of Saxe-Coburg-Gotha, sub- sequently King of the Belgians, perhaps wary of the explosive character of Greek politics, tactfully declined the crown. In due course it rested on the head of Prince Otto, son of King Ludwig of Bavaria, a true philhellene. But Otto failed to satisfy the people's fanatical ambitions to conquer the Turks and regain the glories of the former Greater Greece. Hoping to achieve the all-conquering march to Constantinople, their spiritual home, Otto had invaded Epirus and Thessaly during the Crimean War, but the Powers intervened and revolution was the aftermath.

As Otto's replacement, the people of Athens clamoured for Prince Alfred, Duke of Edinburgh, but neither Queen Victoria nor her government was willing to let Affie risk possible humiliation. In the end, all concerned agreed to accept the matriarch's own nominee, Prince William, the brother of Alexandra of Denmark, her future daughter-in-law. Thus William, then a callow cadet from the Copenhagen naval school and quite uninitiated into the complexities of statecraft, founded that offshoot of the Schleswig-Holstein-Sonderburg-Glücksburg line that supplied monarchs to Greece.

On 30 October 1863 the eighteen-year-old Willy, now known as King George I after the Greek national saint, saw his realm for the first time. As the coaches crunched over the stony plain from the Piraeus to the capital, Athens loomed before him. The Acro- polis brooded over the city, and gunfire boomed down from Acropolis Hill. The Old Palace, to which the Greeks raucously welcomed their young sovereign, chilled even the doughty Danish heart. Stretching down one side of Kifissia Road – the more affluent quarter – the draughty marble halls possessed scant heating, and only certain rooms were heated by enamel stoves.

Amid pungent incense and impressive ritual, King George was crowned the next day, then took his oath in the Athens Assembly. Mr Horace Rumbold, the British chargé d'affaires, who witnessed the ceremony, recorded long afterwards: '... he looked so young and artless that the experiment seemed to all of us questionable and indeed highly hazardous.' Despite his youth, George I was fully aware that he was among unscrupulous politicians – 'many of whom had been steeped to the lips in treason', as Rumbold claimed. George humorously enlightened his ministers that he 'kept a portmanteau ready packed' and would quit Greece if the people rejected him. This proved to be a sensible attitude in years to come.

As a means of stabilizing the throne, King George acquired a Russian wife – the young Grand Duchess Olga, the Tsar's niece. One day their son Christopher would write: 'The bride was such a child that she brought a whole family of dolls with her to her new country. For the entry into Athens she wore a little dress in the Greek colours of blue and white, and the crowds in the streets shouted themselves hoarse in welcome. Her shy youth and beauty conquered their impressionable hearts that day and, through all the vicissitudes of our house, she at least never lost their love.'

George and Olga – the paternal grandparents of Prince Philip, Duke of Edinburgh – founded the Royal House of Greece. Their first child, a son, was christened Constantine by popular demand, after the last Emperor of Byzantine Greece. The ecstatic people saw in the young Prince a portent of a glorious future, which created an impossible burden that would haunt the royal family down the years.

Meanwhile, a native-born family grew: after Constantine came George, Nicholas, Andrew (destined to be Prince Philip's father) and Alexandra and Marie; Olga, born in 1881, died the same year. For everyone in the Old Palace life was spartan. Many years later, during exile, Prince Christopher would write:

There was only one bathroom in the whole place, and no one had ever been known to take a bath in it, for the simple reason that the taps would scarcely ever run and, on the rare occasions when they could be coaxed into doing so, emitted a thin trickle of water in which the corpses of defunct roaches and other strange animals floated dismally .... The cold of the Palace was almost unbearable. The wind whistled down the corridors and curled like a lash in and out of the lofty salons.

To derive greater comfort, in 1871 the King bought an estate of pine woods and heather-clad hills at Tatoi at the foot of Mount Parnes. Constructed in the English Elizabethan style, the mansion overlooked forest slopes across the Attic Plain to the Saronic Gulf. A refuge from the stridence and treachery of Greek politics, the royal family lived in peace, especially in the summer months, roaming over its many acres – the domain of stag, boar and, until they were exterminated, wolf – or ride in yellow Viennese carriages along the many miles of highway cut through the pines. Yet one could not escape from the hatred and vendettas for long. King George once remarked: 'I feel as though I am living on the top of a volcano.'

Marriage to other European dynasties would exacerbate the political hazards. Constantine, the Diadoch or Crown Prince, married in 1889 Princess Sophie Dorothea of Prussia, the grand-daughter of Queen Victoria and sister of the Kaiser William II, a connection which would reverberate seriously on the Greek royal family in the First

Countess Mountbatten with her daughter Pamela, who married David Hicks, the interior designer.

In November 1923 Lord Louis's sister Lady Louise Mountbatten, married the Crown Prince Gustav Adolf of Sweden. On her husband's accession in October 1950 she became Queen of Sweden.

Princess Alice, a great-grand-daughter of Queen Victoria, and the daughter of Prince Louis of Battenberg, married Prince Andrew of Greece.

World War. Alexandra, the King's eldest daughter, married the Grand Duke Paul of Russia in the same year. Thirteen years elapsed before Nicholas took the Grand Duchess Helen of Russia as his bride (one of their daughters, Marina, would eventually become Duchess of Kent). In 1903, Prince Andrew married Princess Alice of Battenberg, and five years later his brother George was joined in matrimony with Princess Marie Bonaparte, a descendant of Napoleon's brother Lucien. Prince Christopher married a wealthy American, Mrs Nancy Leeds, in 1920, and after her death he married again – this time Princess Françoise of France, sister of the Count of Paris. King George's second daughter, like her sister, took a Russian spouse – the Grand Duke George Mihailovich.

Princess Alice of Battenberg was seventeen and Prince Andrew, an officer in the Greek army, twenty when they attended the coronation of King Edward VII in 1902. But they had met earlier at Darmstadt where, for a while, Andrew had been attached to the Hessian 23rd Dragoon Guards. The regimen set for Prince Andrew by his martinet father had been exacting, for George I did not believe in pampering his offspring even in early childhood. Discipline became even more rigid when Andrew, entering the Athens military school, came under the surveillance of German officers. King George I selected the Greek Major Panayotis Danglis as his military tutor, then unaware that his choice would one day treacherously attack the monarchy. For the time being, however, Danglis was ostensibly a royalist, the loyal soldier, who, as an expert in ballistics, had designed a highly effective mountain-gun which, attached to the back of a mule, could be assembled rapidly – a fantastic improvement on the antiquated weaponry which the Greeks hauled by means of men and bullocks over difficult terrain.

Princess Alice had entered this world at Windsor Castle in the same bed in which her own mother, Princess Victoria, had been born. On the night of 24 January 1885 Victoria had slept fitfully in the Tapestry Room. Early the next day, the Queen found her grand-daughter to be 'very suffering' and, with Prince Louis of Battenberg, stayed with her 'till at length, at 20m to 5 in the afternoon, the child, a little girl, was born ... Baby is very small, thin and dark,' recorded the Queen, and on the next day added that she was 'very pretty'.

The Queen had insisted that the birth should take place at Windsor, for the matriarch spoke disparagingly of German gynaecologists; indeed, the withered arm of Prince William of Prussia – the future Kaiser – was ample testimony of their incompetence. But unfortunately Alice would be born with an impediment. For some while Princess Victoria believed her first-born to be slow-witted and disobedient, for she wrote to the Queen: 'The child ... is very lively & quick with her fingers, but decidedly backward of speech, using all sorts of self-invented words and pronouncing others very indistinctly.' Princess Julie of Battenberg was the person who first suspected deafness as the cause of the child's behaviour – a diagnosis which was confirmed by an ear specialist in Darmstadt. In London another specialist went further: the cause of almost entire deafness was a thickening of the Eustachian tubes; an operation would be futile. Alice was therefore taught to lip-read and eventually was conversant in German, English, French and Greek.

It has been implied that the restrictive world of Victorian punctiliousness and Darmstadt provincialism which Alice inhabited – plus her deafness – all the more endeared her to the lively Greek cavalry officer who sported a monocle. It has been claimed, however, that in the initial stages her family were lukewarm to the proposed union. Prince Andrew had little money. Princess Alexandra of Greece, the former Queen of Yugoslavia and cousin of Prince Philip, has asserted that the 'doting great-uncle, King Edward VII . . . declared bluffly that no throne in Europe was too good for her', adding that 'it may be that the King raised an eye-brow at an unpromising match to a younger son – indeed, the youngest but one – of the comparatively new Royal House of the Hellenes.' If this is true, Edward VII must have changed his view. During May 1903, when the engagement was officially announced, Prince Andrew was invited to London. Princess Victoria related: 'His engagement to Alice was announced by Uncle Bertie at a family dinner given by George and May [Prince and Princess of Wales] at Marlborough House at a sort of housewarming party . . . Very shy he was on the day that he, Alice and I assisted at a Te Deum in honour of the engagement at the Greek Church, which was followed by a reception at the [Greek] legation.'

The *Daily Express* informed its readers: '. . . it is stated that several imperial and royal relatives have between them generously contributed sufficient funds to enable the young people to start life without excessive financial sorrows. A wedding present from the Tsar of £100,000 was the largest contribution.'

Maybe he was influenced because it was the traditional venue, but Prince Louis of Battenberg, then Director of Naval Intelligence at the British Admiralty, chose Darmstadt as the setting for his daughter's wedding, on 7 October 1903. Hesse was certainly central for the many foreign guests. The occasion demonstrated how very close the links between the Battenbergs and Europe's reigning houses were. Queen Alexandra, with the Princesses Victoria and Beatrice, represented King Edward VII; Tsar Nicholas and his family, who brought the Imperial Russian Choir to sing national songs and Gregorian tunes, displayed Romanoff pomp; Grand Duke Paul and Ella and Serge were among the Russian contingent, and King George and Queen Olga of Greece, Prince Andrew's parents, attended with their family. The galaxy of guests included the Kaiser's brother, Prince Henry of Prussia, and his wife Princess Irene, and a cross-section of minor royalties from all over Germany. Austrian archdukes and Danish and French princes also arrived with their suites, and the Battenberg party included a nanny with a boy of three, the future Earl Mountbatten of Burma. Many would be consumed in the conflagration of war and subsequent revolution, but on that delightful autumn day they lived in a secure and carefree world.

For Princess Alice the domestic scene in Hesse differed greatly from the cheerless Old Palace in Athens, but there was comfort and relaxation at Tatoi. Gradually children were born: Margarita in 1905 and Theodora the next year; Cecilie arrived in 1911, and Sophie three years later. Not until 10 June 1921 would Prince Philip be born, at the villa called 'Mon Repos' on Corfu. Princess Alice interested herself in the School of Greek Embroidery, learning the intricacies of the national craft, while Prince Andrew continued his military career. Life was orderly, but one could not dismiss the intermittent political smouldering nor the Military League led by revolutionary-minded men like General Theodore Pangalos. The King's powers were being eroded, and in his Prime Minister, Eleutherios Venizelos, George I saw the threat of republicanism.

In 1909, Prince Andrew and his brothers were forced, because of political intrigue, to resign their commissions in both the army and the navy, but three years later war temporarily united the factions. Greece had remained outside the military treaty signed by Serbia, Bulgaria and Montenegro against the loathed Turks, yet from the balcony at the Old Palace, in September 1912, King George, with Prince Andrew holding a candle beside him, read the order for general mobilization. Below, the street lights in Kifissia Square picked out the milling crowds who, amid a cacophony of tram bells, motor horns and tin cans, demonstrated their approval. By 8 October the Greek Army, commanded by Crown Prince Constantine, had assembled at Larissa. Greek fury so mutilated the Turkish forces that on 11 November, King George – accompanied by Princess Alice, who had brought much-needed medical supplies – entered Salonika in a downpour of rain. His victory was short lived. Walking unguarded among the people – a practice he had developed in Athens – he was shot dead by a Macedonian Greek. The motive was never known.

An unstable throne was Constantine's inheritance – a state of affairs which also affected Andrew and Alice. Crisis rose to its peak with the fatal shots fired at Sarajevo and the bloodbath of the First World War. King Constantine in vain professed neutrality, a claim which was treated cynically by the Allies, because his consort was the Kaiser's sister. The pro-Allied Venizelos resigned and founded his revolutionary committee in Salonika. Espionage festered in Athens, and daylight exposed in the streets the bodies of many murdered by revolutionary elements. Rumours were wild and rampant. The King and Queen almost lost their lives at Tatoi in a forest fire, reputed to be the nefarious plot of Allied agents, and Constantine was alleged to be radioing reports to the Germans with equipment secreted among the trees. Although it had been constructed in 1894, the King was even accused of building a landing-stage at 'Mon Repos' so that German U-boats could refuel.

Desperately trying to reassure the Allies, in July 1916 Constantine despatched his brothers Andrew and Nicholas to tell them the truth. Both Princess Alice and Prince Andrew lacked German sympathies, yet in Britain Andrew met with ugly rumours. London newspapers accused him of intriguing with Constantine's Prime Minister Gounaris and Colonel Metaxas, as well as Count Mirbach, the former German ambassador in Athens, and the Kaiser's emissary Baron von Schenk, who 'had paid substantial sums of money to stir up trouble against the Allies in Greece'. The Allied bombardment of Athens was the final humiliation.

Prince Andrew and Princess Alice, with the rest of the royal family, were exiled to Switzerland after the war, where they lived in a state of constant anxiety. Prince Christopher wrote years later:

We lived in Switzerland for the next three years, spending our summers in Zurich and Lucerne and our winters at St Moritz. It was a hand-to-mouth existence with its daily worries over ways and means. Our private incomes were stopped, and we had to depend on borrowed money ... Just when we were wondering where in the world the next quarter's rent was coming from, someone always stepped into the breach ... As political exiles we were regarded as dangerous and suspicious characters, and our friends could only visit us in the strictest secrecy, for we were subject to a rigid espionage and had all our correspondence censored.

Alexander, Constantine's son, had been left on the throne as a puppet sovereign manipulated by the Venizelos clique, an abasement which ended abruptly in 1920. Visiting his vineyard keeper at Tatoi, he was fatally bitten by one of two pet monkeys which had attacked his Alsatian dog. Venizelos was already at war with the Turks in Anatolia and now foolishly imagined that it was opportune to proclaim a republic. Quite unexpectedly, in a plebiscite, the majority of the people voted – to the chagrin of Britain and France – to have ex-King Constantine recalled. Whitehall and the Quai d'Orsay stressed to the Greeks that 'the restoration of a King whose disloyal attitude during the War had caused grave embarrassment, must be regarded as ratification by Greece of his hostile attitude'.

A dangerous situation was being created for Constantine. Venizelos's obsession to win back the Greater Greece and establish Hellenic republicanism had bred economic disaster. Constantine could not evade this inheritance. Moreover, without Anglo-French political support and financial aid, nothing could avoid disaster. Hostilities had gone too far. It was imperative to satisfy national pride; furthermore, to withdraw from Asia Minor would expose the Greek nationals there to large-scale massacre. Much against his inclination, Constantine had to continue the war. A reluctant Prince Andrew, chosen to represent the royal family in the field, commanded an army corps to bolster morale.

For Andrew the outcome was catastrophic. During August 1922, the world's press reported Greek defeat by Mustapha Kemel, the founder of new Turkey. Rioting and panic characterized the retreat. At Smyrna Greeks were slaughtered, burned or drowned in an orgy of death. Scapegoats had to be found to account for such ignominy. Disastrously for Prince Andrew, his troops had been the first to wilt then crack under the Turkish onslaught, yet he argued that the calamity was the result of crass incompetence; the more efficient weaponry which Danglis, his former tutor, had invented, was conspicuously absent. At his own request, he was relieved of his command on 22 July 1922, and in October returned with his family to 'Mon Repos'.

The Prince's resentment for the incompetence and intrigues of the politicians and general staff was expressed eloquently in his letter, dated 22 July 1921, to General Papoulas, the commander-in-chief. He alleged that the brigade of mountain artillery had been sent only after his repeated requests, but its 'personnel was so ignorant that for days it was unable even to find the Division, in spite of all my instructions. It was so untrained that in yesterday's action at Alpanos, in which the Division fought for six hours against a strongly entrenched force of 8,000 men, only four guns of one battery supported the attack. The brigade, during the whole of the action, was engaged in making endless reconnaissances, and when it did fire once, it fired at our own troops.'

In the unstable aftermath of war, King Constantine quit the throne, in favour of his son George who, until Greece became a republic on 1 May 1923, was a mere pawn of the military dictators Plastiros and Pangalos. Andrew had been assured by the revolutionaries that he would be left undisturbed at Corfu, but, in October 1922, soon after rejoining his family, he was conveyed by a destroyer to the mainland – summoned to a court of the revolutionary committee in Athens. Misled into believing that he was to give evidence against the 'royal traitors', Prince Andrew was instead indicted of high treason and committed to gaol. Fellow inmates were three ex-Prime Ministers and a number of ministers and military officers, all accused of being the architects of Greek reversals during the war.

When the first of the trials ended, Demetrios Gounaris and five others died before shooting-squads on 13 November. The trial of Prince Andrew and five generals had been arranged for 2 December. It is said that the Prince had resigned himself to execution. Death, indeed, might have been his fate but for the courage and determination of Princess Alice. Entrusting her children to others, she hurried to Athens, then, at personal risk, sought the intervention of the Pope, King Alfonso of Spain and her two brothers in London. Lord Louis Mountbatten approached King George V for help, then talked with Bonar Law, the Prime Minister. The attendance of Lord Curzon, the Foreign Secretary, at the League of Nations in Geneva, at first caused some delay. To any dispassionate observer it must have appeared illogical that, after vehemently condemning the 'German Greeks', a Foreign Office telegram now disclosed that the King 'is most anxious concerning Prince Andrew. Please report on His Royal Highness's present position, and continue to keep us informed by telegraph of any development.'

Returning to Athens, Andrew's younger brother Christopher made strenuous but abortive efforts to save the Prince's life. Describing his experiences later he wrote:

No one was allowed to go near Andrew except his valet. Guards kept strictest watch and confiscated all letters and parcels. Finally I hit on the expedient of writing a letter on cigarette paper, rolling it tightly and putting it with cigarettes into his valet's case. Andrew answered it with a short note, full of courage, but . . . I knew that he had no longer any hope of regaining freedom. He had just had a conversation with a former school-fellow, Pangalos, now Minister of War and instigator of his trial, that left him small grounds for optimism. Plastiras, incidentally, had served under Prince Andrew in the disastrous campaign.

'How many children have you?' Pangalos had asked suddenly, and when my brother told him, he shook his head: 'Poor things, what a pity, they will soon be orphans!'

The British, fortunately, were not inactive. Commander Gerald Talbot, then serving in the British foreign service and at one time Britain's naval attaché in the Greek capital, was briefed by Curzon to get Prince Andrew and his family out of Greece. Using false papers, he reached Athens on 28 November, some days ahead of the trial. If, as has been claimed, it is true that Talbot was scheming to abduct the Prince, such clandestine methods were unnecessary after he had spoken to Pangalos. On 30 November, in the early hours of the morning, a message, telegraphed from the British Legation in Athens to the Foreign Office in London, read:

... Mr Talbot has obtained this evening a promise from Minister of War and also from Colonel Plastiras, the two leaders of government, that Prince Andrew will not be executed but allowed to leave the country in charge of Mr Talbot. Following is the arrangement agreed upon:

Prince will be tried on Saturday and sentenced to penal servitude or possibly to death. Plastiras will then grant pardon and hand him over to Mr Talbot for immediate removal with Princess by British warship to Brindisi or to any other port en route to England. British warship must be at Phaleron by midday December 3rd and captain should report immediately to legation for orders, but in view of necessity for utmost secrecy, captain should be given no indication of reason for voyage.

This promise has been obtained with greatest difficulty and Talbot is convinced that above arrangement be strictly adhered to so as to save Prince's life. As success of plan depends on absolute secrecy of existence of this arrangement, even Prince and Princess cannot be given hint of coming. Talbot is convinced that he can rely on word given him, and I see of no other possibility of saving Prince's life.

The military court found Prince Andrew guilty of the disgrace of disobeying orders and abandoning his post, sentencing him to imprisonment, deprivation of rank and titles and banishment from Greece for life. 'But consideration being given to extenuating circumstances of lack of experience in commanding a large unit, he has been degraded and condemned to perpetual banishment.' The words would be etched deeply on his mind. It appears, indeed, that they soured him appreciably for the rest of his life. (When documents of British foreign policy from 1919 to 1939 were due to be published, this and an earlier telegram announcing Talbot's efforts to rescue the royal prisoner were submitted to Sir Michael Adeane, then Queen Elizabeth's private secretary, for fear there might be some objection to their being printed. Prince Philip objected only to an editor's footnote relating to the verdict. He recommended in a brief message its deletion: 'People might think it was true.')

Andrew's fellow-prisoners were condemned and executed. Pangalos called at the prison during the night and personally drove the more fortunate Prince, accompanied by Talbot, to the cruiser *Calypso* to be reunited with Princess Alice. At Corfu their four daughters and the baby Prince Philip, in the arms of his nanny, Miss Roose, were conveyed to the ship. Not for many years would the infant Philip appreciate the drama of recent weeks and the significance of exile. In the pattern of his life it would be seen that politics, revolution and ancestry were the cardinal threads.

On the voyage to Brindisi, sailors lined an orange crate for use as a cot – his introduction to the Royal Navy.

11

Controversy Over a Name

HAVING reached the sanctuary of London, the royal exiles resided for a while with Princess Alice's mother, Princess Victoria, now the Dowager Marchioness of Milford Haven, at Kensington Palace. In the years to come this grace-and-favour apartment would become more familiar to the fair-haired, blue-eyed Philip. So, too, would two Mountbatten uncles: George, the talented second Marquess of Milford Haven, and his younger brother, Lord Louis. Moreover, the child's temporary separation from his parents would be a pointer to the future. In the New Year, Prince Andrew and Princess Alice journeyed to New York to visit Prince Christopher and his wife (the widow of the American millionaire William B. Leeds), before cruising in their yacht from Canada to Palm Beach.

On their return, Prince Andrew was confronted with the immediate task of maintaining his family. His cousin, King Christian X of Denmark, had issued the family with Danish passports, but there was the inexorable question of finance. It is on record – but, like many stories involving the British royal family, it may be apocryphal – that King George V brusquely announced that he would 'not pay for any extravagance Andrew might indulge in' – a curt refusal which, so it is said, induced Princess Beatrice to provide for the exiles, at least temporarily. His property and army pay now confiscated, Andrew's means were limited. To his aid came two family benefactors – Uncle George of Milford Haven and Andrew's brother George. But if Prince Philip's cousin Alexandra is correct, George Milford Haven's contribution 'scarcely met the schooling expenses of the girls'. George had inherited his father's titles but no outstanding wealth; furthermore, the Bolsheviks had divested his wife, the daughter of the Grand Duke Michael of Russia, of her wealth.

For Prince George of Greece, however, there was no fear of financial stringency. He had married Princess Marie Bonaparte who had inherited an enormous fortune from maternal ancestors; Marie Blanc, whom her father Prince Roland Bonaparte had married, was the daughter of the man who founded the casino at Monte Carlo. Consequently, to leave London for Paris and avail himself of the generosity of the granddaughter of Francois Blanc, was the most practical thing for Prince Andrew to do. Thus indirectly the gold francs from the roulette tables helped Prince Philip's family in the early years of banishment.

First they occupied rooms in a huge mansion owned by Prince George and Princess Marie in the Rue Adolph Ivan, close to the Bois de Boulogne, then moved to another property – which was again made available by Uncle George and Aunt Marie – at St Cloud. This was the domestic scene which Prince Philip regarded as his childhood home. His grandmother, Princess Victoria, visited them, and she and the family embarked on excursions to relatives in Germany and Sweden, or to Roumania to stay with Queen Helen and her son Michael, the future sovereign and Prince Philip's cousin.

During the autumn of 1924, Princess Alice was staying at Kensington Palace with her mother when it was decided to have Philip brought from Paris to London. Alice met him at Victoria Station and found her son 'very excited & pleased'. She also revealed that Philip 'discovered the first policeman by himself & pointed him out to me. Also the buses were his joy, & I had to take him in one this afternoon. Of course he made straight for the top, but it was too windy and showery to go there, but he was reasonable and went inside . . .'

The impression of a sad and neglected child is quite ridiculous and misleading. Apart from his parents, there was the affection of his sisters who were years older than himself. In fact this ash-blond little extrovert was at ease with all kinds of people. Many hours of happiness were also given by Madame Foufounis, a Greek exile and one of Princess Alice's friends, who was then residing at the Villa Georges, a beautiful country house with its own farm near Marseilles. There he enjoyed the companionship of her children – Ria, Hélène (today Madame Hélène Cordet) and their brother Ianni – and when they were taken for holidays at Berck Plage near Le Touquet, Philip and Miss Roose and his sisters would sometimes accompany them.

Madame Cordet, today recalling vignettes of childhood, has confessed that, although she liked Philip, she was irritated – much to his amusement – by the fuss her mother, by then a widow, made of him. Even so, they had 'a wonderful time playing soldiers, growing vegetables and fruit on our little plot of land (given to us so that we would keep out of mischief) and feeding the animals on the farm. Philip's great distraction was cleaning the pigsties.'

Due to a hip complaint, Ria was encased in plaster when she was seven years old, and remained incapacitated for five years. While at Berck Plage a friend bought toys for all except the unfortunate Ria. He explained rather clumsily: 'I didn't get you anything because you can't play like the others.' Philip stared silently while Ria tried to suppress her tears, then ran off to his room. Minutes later he returned, clutching his own toys as well as the new one. 'All this is yours,' he explained, placing them on Ria's bed. He was only four years old. Always considerate, Philip would frequently sit chatting to Ria.

There would be times, however, when there was uproar in the house followed by a necessary spanking. Ianni received his beating from Miss Macdonald, a formidable Scottish governess, called 'Auntie', when he and Philip broke a huge vase. Philip thought

Prince Andrew and Princess
Alice of Greece at Berck
Plage in France with their
son, Prince Philip, then four
years old.

The young Prince Philip
with his invalid friend Ria
Foufounis and two of his
sisters, Cecile and 'Tiny'.

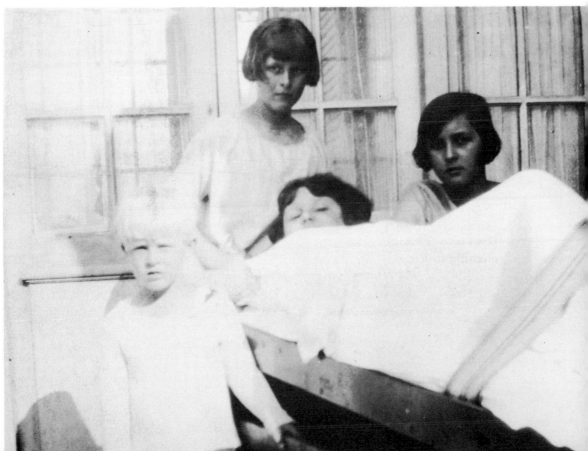

it expedient to dash away, then suddenly his frightened eyes were seen behind french windows, and in a panic he cried: 'Nanny, let's clear!' Yet when Auntie descended on Philip, he straightened himself, looked her clearly in the eye, and said: 'I will get my spanking from Roosie, thank you.'

Childhood had other moments of pain. Pretending, for instance, that they were keeping a dental appointment, Ianni and Philip went to a circus instead. The young Hélène, mad with fury at being deceived, turned on both, her eyes flashing. Ianni ran quickly out of reach, but Philip merely stood as if fascinated by her anger. She grabbed him by his hair, not letting go until finally she was left with tufts in each hand.

Philip received his earliest education at the MacJannet Country Day and Boarding School at St Cloud, a progressive kindergarten founded by a graduate of Tufts College, Massachusetts, for the children of rich Americans residing in France. More commonly known as The Elms (because it existed in an old mansion of that name), the MacJannet School asked high fees, which in Philip's case were paid by his American aunt.

It was during this phase of his childhood that Princess Alice began to reveal the religious traits of her Aunt Ella and a desire to help the unfortunate. She started 'Hellas', a modest boutique, in which she sold Greek embroidery, tapestries and other articles to help Greek expatriots. Regrettably, exile marked the gradual drifting apart of Philip's parents. The mortifying ordeal of the Athens trial had left Prince Andrew extremely bitter – 'intrancible, his equanimity in tatters'. Air Vice-Marshal Arthur S. Gould Lee, who enjoyed the confidence of members of the Greek royal family, wrote that Prince Andrew was 'unable to forgive the way in which, after long years of honest military service, he had been subjected to public insult and indignity for the sins of others'. Probably, too, Princess Alice's obsession with religion and her overpowering desire to assist the needy angered him. One must also appreciate that some of the events in Greece and exile had severely taxed both nerves and stamina. Now, for some years, Alice would have to resort to periods of treatment in German and Swiss sanatoria.

Did this tacit breach leave its mark on Philip? Both parents mutually agreed that he should never be exposed to the sort of outrage that Prince Andrew had suffered. It was agreed, therefore, that he should live with Princess Victoria in England, and that Uncle George should act as guardian. Time would indicate that Uncle Louis and Theodora, the boy's sister, would – wittingly or not – also greatly mould the pattern of Philip's destiny. Victoria's apartments at Kensington Palace were too limiting for a lively, boisterous boy, and so he was transferred to Lynden Manor, his Uncle George's Thames-side home near Maidenhead. Here, too, was the companionship of his cousin David, his senior by two years.

With Prince Andrew's consent, Philip was sent to Cheam, England's oldest preparatory school, to which Prince Louis of Battenberg, then the First Sea Lord, had sent his son George. For the holidays, during the whole of his school life in Britain, Philip had a variety of addresses at which to stay. Among them were Lynden Manor, Kensington Palace, Brook House or Adsdean (with Uncle Louis) and the home of Harold

George, the second Marquess of Milford Haven (on the right) at Cowes with (left to right) Count Michael de Torby, the Marchioness (formerly Countess Nada de Torby), and Princess Margarita, the elder sister of Prince Philip, Duke of Edinburgh.

Lady Milford Haven, with her son David, who became the third Marquess, and daughter, Lady Tatiana Mountbatten.

Wernher, a millionaire business man, who had married Lady Anastasia ('Zia') Torby, the sister of Nada, Uncle George's wife.

His mentor, Uncle George, a naval officer of immense charm and intelligence, must have influenced Philip's character in those impressionable years. This gifted tactician was at his happiest in a warship, but his restricted inheritance and naval pay were inadequate to maintain Lynden Manor and his wife Nada and her Russian grand ducal tastes. Philip was still at Cheam when, in 1932, having attained the rank of captain, his uncle resigned to seek richer prizes in commerce – first on the New York Stock Exchange and then, as well as taking a smattering of directorships, with an American gyroscope company.

By now Philip had no family to return to at St Cloud. His four sisters had married into German princely families, and within a decade war would place him and his sisters on conflicting sides. Sophie, the youngest, was the first to wed, marrying the thirty-year-old Prince Christopher of Hesse, the youngest brother of Prince Maximillian who, as a nineteen-year-old lieutenant in the Prussian Death's Head Hussars in the First World War, was fatally wounded at Flanders by British cavalry. (This great-grandson of Queen Victoria had requested a doctor at a British hospital at Bailleul to send a locket to his mother in Germany. Unfortunately, three days after Maximillian's death the doctor was also killed when the hospital was blasted by a German shell. Luckily the doctor had already written a note, and the locket was duly received by Queen Mary in England. In time Philip's aunt, Princess Louise of Battenberg, sent it to Maximillian's mother, Princess Margaret of Hesse.)

To the Mountbattens' great embarrassment, three years after his marriage Prince Christopher accepted Nazism in its entirety, joining Himmler's staff in Berlin before volunteering for flying duties in Goering's Luftwaffe. The pilot-prince dropped bombs on London but lost his life in Italy in a similar sortie in 1944. Sophie was then twenty-nine, with four young children; a fifth was born after her husband's death. Eventually she married Prince George of Hanover, augmenting her family with three more children.

Prince Philip's four sisters were all married in the early 1930s. After Sophie's wedding, Cecilie was married to her first cousin once removed, the Grand Duke George Donatus of Hesse. Margarita, the eldest, married Prince Gottfried von Hohenlöhe-Langenburg, a grandson of Prince Alfred, Duke of Edinburgh, and Theodora became the wife of Berthold, Margrave of Baden, a union which influenced Prince Philip's career.

Prince Max of Baden, Theodora's father-in-law, had been the last Chancellor of Imperial Germany. Desperately trying to save his throne, the Kaiser had besought him to seek from the Allies an 'armistice of honour'. Prince Max, however, took the view that only the Kaiser's withdrawal and the destruction of the Prussian military clique could satisfy the Allies. He therefore proclaimed the Kaiser's abdication even before the autocratic William had been warned. Making way for Ebert, the Socialist, Prince Max proclaimed the republic, then surrendered to the Allies.

Prince Philip at Gordonstoun, the school then directed by Dr Kurt Hahn, which Prince Charles would also attend.

Through the marriage of Prince Philip to Princess Elizabeth in November 1947, the Mountbattens were joined inextricably to the British reigning house.

At Schloss Salem, his estate on the forested shores of Lake Constance, Prince Max founded a unique school whose aim was to create a new élite – a German intelligentsia purged of Junker militarism – from the wreckage of war. To supervise his school he appointed Dr Kurt Hahn, his political adviser during his chancellorship, who had been a member of the German delegation at Versailles and collaborated in drafting the constitution of the Weimar Republic.

Encouraged by his sister, Philip became one of Hahn's pupils at Salem, but with the rise of Nazism Hahn was condemned as 'a decadent Jewish corrupter of German youth'. Falsely accused of being a Communist, he was gaoled, and on his release quit Salem and resurrected his school at Gordonstoun. Philip was among the nucleus of Salem pupils and masters to travel to Scotland.

During vacations, the young Prince sometimes visited his sisters in Germany, where occasionally Prince Andrew arranged a rendezvous as well. Father and son met in a further reunion in November 1936, after a plebiscite restored the monarchy in Greece. Philip's uncle and aunt, King Constantine and Queen Sophie, and his paternal grandmother, Queen Olga, had died in exile in the republican era, and arrangements were now made to convey them from a crypt in Florence and inter them in the royal burial ground at Tatoi after lying in state for six days in Athens Cathedral. Princess Alice was unable to attend, for she was still recuperating from a heart complaint in a Swiss nursing-home. But she was residing in Athens when both Philip and his father attended the wedding of the future King Paul I, then Crown Prince of Greece, to the vivacious Princess Frederika of Brunswick. Determined to devote herself to charitable work, Princess Alice now lived with Madame Socopol, an elderly companion, and a maid in Kolonaki Square. In her house many signed photographs recalled her Battenberg connection.

This was the time, it is said, when pressure was applied to effect Philip's enlistment at the Greek Nautical College with the hint of rapid promotion in the Hellenic navy. But Philip declined to yield to enticement, returning to Gordonstoun for his final year.

This period was memorable for two personal tragedies. First Philip learned from Dr Hahn that his sister Cecilie and her husband had died on their way to the wedding in London of Prince Louis of Hesse and the Honourable Margaret Campbell-Geddes. Flying in fog, their plane crashed into a factory chimney at Ostend, killing all on board. Those who died included the Grand Duchess Eleonore of Hesse, the bridegroom's mother, and Prince Philip's two small nephews, Louis and Alexander of Hesse.

The other lamentable loss to Philip was the death of the Marquess of Milford Haven, who had virtually served in the capacity of foster-father. Then only forty-six, Uncle George was a victim of cancer.

Lord Louis Mountbatten now served *in loco parentis* for Prince Andrew. Uncle Louis – the flamboyant destroyer commander, the dynamic aristocrat – would exert a fundamental influence on his nephew from now onwards. Indeed, there would be some remarkable parallels. In character they would both reveal a fearless candour and facility for rousing controversy. Both would follow naval careers which at times would bear some resemblance to that of their respective father and grandfather, Prince Louis of Battenberg. Maltese associations and enthusiasm for polo would be common to all three.

The Hessian connection with Malta was deep rooted. Frederick, the son of the Landgrave Louis V of Hesse, had commanded the galleys of the Knights of Malta against the Turks in 1640 and as captain-general of the island occupied the palace which became Admiralty House. Some three centuries later, Lord Mountbatten and Prince Philip served in precisely the same quarters; there, Lord Louis commanded the First Cruiser Squadron. Another Royal Naval link was through George of Hesse, the son of the Landgrave Louis VI, who commanded the Royal Marines at the capture of Gibraltar and was appointed its governor in 1704.

Lord Mountbatten, it is believed, arranged for Prince Philip to participate in the examination for the Royal Naval College at Dartmouth as a special-entry cadet from a public school. Because of his self-reliance, intelligence and natural leadership, there is every indication that, but for the intervention of his marriage, Prince Philip would have risen – like Uncle Dickie and Grandfather Louis before him – to the supreme hierarchy of the navy. It is not an assessment, however, of his naval career but his status in the British royal family which is of significance to this book.

When rumours of the romance between Prince Philip and Princess Elizabeth gained substance, King George VI appreciated that Philip was both a member of the provocative Greek monarchy and an alien. Because of the war, many Britons were resentful towards foreigners. To them anyone from an established British family was preferable to the most distinguished names in the *Almanach de Gotha*. Indeed, the King himself had married a commoner and shunned the tradition whereby members of the British royal family contracted marriage with foreign brides and bridegrooms. When forty per cent of those questioned in an opinion poll voted against the choice of Philip as Princess Elizabeth's suitor, George VI had to take note. Reports, however, implied that King George of the Hellenes and Lord Mountbatten disregarded public attitude and used their influence in Philip's favour. It has been claimed that Lord Mountbatten's overriding passion was to break down any obstruction to Philip's engagement to the heiress to the British throne. In his official biography of King George VI John W. Wheeler-Bennet wrote categorically that 'as far back as 1944 four years before Elizabeth's marriage, Lord Mountbatten was urging his nephew's desire'.

But the situation in Greece did not help. There, a tottering throne was shored up precariously by British troops, whose backing for an allegedly cruel administration created international friction. In Britain the Socialist Party – and even the Attlee cabinet – was in conflict. Publically expressing their horror over events in Greece, eighty-six left-wing backbenchers condemned the Greek royal régime for 'barbaric atrocities'. Even if the claim was exaggerated, the political climate was not ideal in which to announce an engagement. To avoid friction, a formula had to be devised. This came in the form of Philip's British naturalization and renunciation of his hereditary claim to the Greek throne. Naturalization raised the question of a surname, for the royal families of Denmark and Greece used no family name. Someone at the College of Heralds suggested the title 'Prince of Oldcastle' – an anglicized version of Oldenburg, the name of the German dukes from whom emanated the Danish royal family. This, however, did not seem appropriate, and, according to one writer, was discordant to Earl Mountbatten's ears.

By now Prince Philip had no father to consult. During the Second World War Prince Andrew had first lived at Cannes on board the yacht *Davida*, aware of the heart complaint that finally killed him. Just before daybreak on 3 December 1944, in a villa loaned to him in Monte Carlo, he rose from his bed, put on his dressing-gown then sat in his armchair and died. No one therefore knew what his reactions would have been to the choice of surname for his son, when King George VI approved the anglicized version of the maiden name of Princess Alice, Philip's mother. Rejecting a British title, the Prince preferred to be known simply as Lieutenant Philip Mountbatten, RN, but by the time of his marriage he would be a duke.

Cynics have argued that Prince Philip is not a Mountbatten. It is fatuous, however, to deny that he is as much the grandson of Prince Louis and Princess Victoria of Battenberg as he is of King George and Queen Olga of Greece. No one, furthermore, can deny the fact that he is the great-grandson of Prince Alexander of Hesse and Princess Julie of Battenberg, the founders of the Battenberg-Mountbatten line.

At a private investiture at Buckingham Palace on 19 November 1947, the eve of the wedding, George VI granted Philip rank and status suitable for the consort of the heiress presumptive by creating him a Knight Commander of the Most Honourable Order of the Garter. (Whether or not he wished to guarantee seniority – an insinuation that has been made – the King had invested Princess Elizabeth eight days earlier.) Sir Philip Mountbatten was then created Duke of Edinburgh, Earl of Merioneth and Baron Greenwich. The choice of dukedom had historic origins, reviving the title which had vanished on the death in 1900 of Affie, Duke of Edinburgh, who had encouraged Philip's maternal grandfather, Prince Louis of Battenberg, to enter the navy. No one has explained why King George VI never created Philip a British prince. Could it really have been an oversight? It has been suggested that it was 'done on the advice of Mr Attlee and others who feared the popular effect of too much too soon'. Queen Elizabeth II would correct the omission a decade later. On 22 February 1957, she declared that the Duke 'shall henceforth be known as His Royal Highness The Prince Philip, Duke of Edinburgh'.

The question of surname was less straightforward. In keeping with normal practice, on her marriage to Philip Mountbatten in 1947 Princess Elizabeth changed her name to that of her husband. Thus, when she ascended the throne, the surname of the royal family was Mountbatten – a name ranking in the thousand-year-old story of the British monarchy with the Plantagenets, Tudors and Stuarts. Yet after two months, the government – reinforced by some public sentiment – insisted that the family name should revert

Beginning with the birth of Prince Charles, heir apparent, Prince Philip is the progenitor of future British sovereigns. The photograph shows Princess Elizabeth holding Princess Anne after the child's christening and the godparents: (left to right, front) Princess Alice, Countess of Athlone (proxy for Princess Alice of Greece) and the Queen Mother; (standing) Earl Mountbatten of Burma, Princess Margarita of Hohenlöhe-Langenburg (Prince Philip's eldest sister), and the Hon. Andrew Elphinstone (first cousin of Princess Elizabeth).

to Windsor. The insinuation persisted that the ambitious Mountbattens had encroached too far on the monarchy and should be checked.

On her accession, there was speculation as to whether the Queen would be the last sovereign of the House of Windsor. It was customary that the death of a queen regnant concluded her dynasty. The question now arose – and was sharply debated – whether Prince Charles, the Queen's heir, would found the House of Mountbatten.

For years the British royal house had been slipshod over the use of a surname; indeed, from the time of Queen Anne – the last of the reigning Stuarts – until the birth of the future King George VI, the family had lacked a surname. When Anne's successor, the German princeling who was crowned George I, came to London from Hanover, he bore no surname. Far in the past, his family had been called Este, Guelph or Wettin, names which had long been dispensed with.

Moreover, at one time all members of the royal family were styled 'Highness'. But in 1917 King George V restricted the use of princely styles to children of the monarch and of the monarch's sons but not of his daughters. Now finding it imperative to adopt a surname for his family, George V decided – because Britain was at war with Germany – against continuing the Prince Consort's family name of Saxe-Coburg-Gotha and instead coined that of Windsor for Queen Victoria's descendants in the male line. The King was anxious that the name should be permanent: 'Determined that henceforth our House and Family shall be styled and known as the House of Windsor.'

On such an issue, an oversight was rather puzzling: that the monarch had not anticipated what would happen if the succession passed to a female. But on this point there was precedent. Queen Victoria was the last Hanoverian. On her death the House of Hanover ended when his heir, having inherited his father's name, introduced the House of Coburg. In like manner, when Prince Charles should succeed Queen Elizabeth II – the last sovereign of the House of Windsor – he would initiate the House of Mountbatten. Yet on 9 April 1952, the *London Gazette* announced: 'The Queen today declared in Council Her Will and Pleasure that She and Her Children shall be styled and known as the House and Family of Windsor, and that Her descendants, other than female descendants who marry, and their descendants who marry, and their descendants, shall bear the name of Windsor.'

To have renounced the dynastic name of Windsor would have been crass folly, for the mere notion of it generated that sense of stability which was instilled into the nation during the reigns of George V and George VI. It was so deeply ingrained and British that it recalled a millennium of national history. But this did not mean that Prince Philip's name should vanish overnight from the royal pedigree. Many people were incensed, their attitude being crystallized by Mr Dermot Morrah, Arundel Herald of Arms Extraordinary, who argued that the ruling 'did less than justice' to Her Majesty's husband 'as the progenitor of the dynasty to come'.

One suspects that the Queen yielded to change under pressure, for Edward S. Iwi, the constitutional lawyer, writing in the *Law Journal* in March 1960, claimed: 'This

There was strident criticism over the hyphenating of the name
Mountbatten with the royal family's name of Windsor. But, as Princess
Anne's marriage certificate shows, this is now a fact.

The naval connection established by Prince Louis of Battenberg has
persisted with the modern Mountbattens. Shown aboard the royal yacht
Britannia at a Jubilee Fleet Review are Prince Philip, his uncle Earl
Mountbatten of Burma and Prince Charles. Also present are the Dukes of
Gloucester and Kent, the Queen and Prince Edward.

[the Family of Mountbatten] continued for only two months because, it is said, as a result of great pressure by Sir Winston Churchill, a change was made.'

It did not appear that the Queen conceded to the politicians too willingly, for on 30 September 1952, the *London Gazette* disclosed: 'The Queen has been graciously pleased by Warrant bearing date the 18th instant to declare and ordain that His Royal Highness Philip Duke of Edinburgh ... shall henceforth upon all occasions ... except where otherwise provided by Act of Parliament have, hold and enjoy Place, Pre-eminence and Precedence next to Her Majesty.' The Queen had elevated her husband to the rank of First Gentleman of the Realm. One derives the impression that the Queen was biding her time, for on 8 February 1960, eleven days before the birth of her third child – the son to be christened Prince Andrew after Prince Philip's father – the Queen reversed the decision taken eight years earlier, declaring in Council that 'while I and my children shall continue to be styled and known as the House and Family of Windsor, my descendants, other than descendants enjoying the style, title or attributes of Royal Highness and the titular dignity of Prince and Princess, and female descendants who marry and their descendants, shall bear the name Mountbatten-Windsor'. To some people this was confusing, but a Buckingham Palace official enlightened them: 'The Queen has always wanted to associate her husband with their descendants. She has had this in mind for a long time, and it is close to her heart.' Critics scoffed that the declaration was virtually pointless since princes and princesses ignored surnames. Constitutional lawyers, however, held that they possessed a 'latent' surname. Yet no one believed that there could be a Mountbatten-Windsor until the third generation from the monarch.

The greatest censure for the decision to combine the name Mountbatten with Windsor occurred in the British press. The *Daily Telegraph* was charitable, contending that 'it was the normal practice of the Queen's subjects that a child uses the name of his father's family, and this personal wish, natural to an expectant mother, had become stronger than ever'. Certain other newspapers were diametrically opposed. The *Daily Mirror*, for example, described it as a 'curious decision', and asked: 'Is the decision prudent? If it is prudent, is it necessary? If it is necessary, is it well timed?' pointing out that 'it is only fifteen years after the Second World War against Germany that the British nation are abruptly informed that the name Mountbatten, formerly Battenberg, is to be joined willy-nilly with the name of Windsor'.

Some newspapers insinuated that it was not so much the Queen's desire as the dark intrigue of the wicked uncle, Earl Mountbatten of Burma, who was possessed with an almost fanatical desire to perpetuate and exalt his name. The *Daily Mirror* wanted to know if the Prime Minister and the cabinet 'were merely informed, or did they agree?', then, dispensing with innuendo forthrightly, claimed that 'Earl Mountbatten was fully aware of what was going on.'

The Queen's declaration, one read in the *Daily Mail*, 'which will hyphenate the newly-forged Mountbatten name indissolubly with the British Crown, can have brought profounder gratification to no one more than Earl Mountbatten, son of Prince Louis of Battenberg, whose name did not ring sweetly in British ears, and uncle of Prince Philip ... certainly the most controversial figure in this forcefully successful family.'

Lord Beaverbrook, that crusader of Empire, who had criticized Earl Mountbatten for his activities on the Indian sub-continent, was as virulent as ever.

One spectre has always confronted Earl Mountbatten of Burma: that his family name should finally die out. For he himself has two daughters now married ... and he has a nephew who is the Marquess of Milford Haven. And another who holds perhaps the greater honour and responsibility than any other member of his ancient family – Prince Philip. Small wonder then that Lord Mountbatten, whose devotion to his heritage is little short of fanatical, has for many years nursed a secret ambition that one day, the name of the ruling House of Britain might be Mountbatten ... Within the conclave of the family, Lord Mountbatten has raised the matter more than once: suggested that even if the name of Windsor be retained, the name of Mountbatten might also be included.

Prince Philip was less concerned than his uncle in the future of the name, though he took pains to see that the Prince of Wales should know of his heritage. He sent over to German genealogists to secure a complete family tree for Prince Charles to see ... Through all this, the Queen remained steadfast in one respect. She could never see the name of Windsor, chosen by her grandfather, abandoned by the royal House. On the other hand, she sympathizes with her husband's feelings – and more particularly with the overtures of his uncle. So, the compromise. Her descendants – though not those who stand in direct line to the Throne – shall carry the name Mountbatten-Windsor.

In time this would be shown to be not the case. Thirteen years later, at her wedding at Westminster Abbey on 14 November 1973, the only daughter of Queen Elizabeth and Prince Philip – herself in direct line to the throne – signed her name in the register 'Anne Mountbatten-Windsor'.

Obviously there is no concrete evidence to prove that Earl Mountbatten induced anyone to change the royal name. As regards his own title, long before the Queen's announcement in February 1960, he had already taken the precaution to ensure his earldom, viscountcy and barony should persist. A 'Special Remainder' was incorporated into his Letter Patent whereby 'in default of heirs male of his body', his title should go 'to his elder daughter and the heirs of her body, and to every other daughter successively in order of seniority of age and priority of birth, and to the heirs of their bodies'.

After that hasty elopement from the Russian Court in October 1851, Prince Alexander of Hesse – in face of many setbacks – created a solid foundation for his descendants. The overbearing Hohenzollerns, and others who treated his morganatic family with disdain, have now vanished into the vagueness of time. But the Battenbergs, or Mountbattens, have come a long, long way. As someone once wrote, the Hesse princes received many renascent transfusions: German and Polish, French and English, Greek and

Hungarian, Jewish and Spanish. In pursuit of their family interest they either allied themselves with, or fought, the Tsars and the Kaisers, the Emperors of France and Austria, Bismarck and the Sultan; they gave a ruler to Bulgaria, queens to Spain and Sweden, a princess to Greece, a husband to a prima donna, two First Sea Lords to Britain, a Viceroy to India, and a husband to the grand-daughter to a Jewish financier, a saleswoman to a New York store, a wife to a London interior designer – and, of course, the present heir to the throne of English kings. But it was the links by marriage to Queen Victoria's descendants that have nurtured and stabilized their status in modern times.

Select Bibliography

Almedingen, E. M., *An Unbroken Unity: A Memoir of Grand Duchess Serge of Russia*, 1964

Aronson, Theo, *Grandmama of Europe*, 1973

D'Auvergne, Edmund B., *The Coburgs*, 1911

Bloom, Ursula, *Princesses in Love*, 1973

Bolitho, Hector, *Further Letters of Queen Victoria*, 1938

Connell, Brian, *Manifest Destiny*, 1953

Cookridge, E. H., *From Battenberg to Mountbatten*, 1966

Duff, David, *Hessian Tapestry*, 1967

Duff, David, *The Shy Princess*, 1958

Earl Mountbatten of Burma, *The Mountbatten Lineage*, 1958

Fjellman, Margit, *Louise Mountbatten, Queen of Sweden*, 1968

Fulford, Roger, *Dearest Mama*, 1968

Hamilton, Gerald, *Blood Royal*, 1964

Hatch, Alden, *The Mountbattens*, 1966

Hough, Richard, *Advice to a Grand-daughter*, 1975

Hough, Richard, *Louis and Victoria*, 1974

Kerr, Mark, *Prince Louis of Battenberg*, 1934

Lee, Arthur S. Gould, *The Royal House of Greece*, 1948

Lowe, Charles, *Prince Bismarck*, 1885

Margutti, Baron von, *The Emperor Franz Joseph and His Times*, 1921

Masson, Madelcine, *Edwina*, 1958

Murphy, Ray, *Last Viceroy*, 1948

Nicolson, Harold, *King George the Fifth*, 1952

Noel, Gerard, *Princess Alice*, 1974

Prince Andrew of Greece, *Towards Disaster – the Greek Army in Asia Minor in 1921*, 1930

Prince Christopher of Greece, *Memoirs*, 1938

Princess Marie Louise, *My Memories of Six Reigns*, 1956

Princess Marie zu Erbach-Schönberg, *Reminiscences*, 1925

Princess Victoria of Prussia, *My Memoirs*, 1929

Queen Alexandra of Yugoslavia, *Prince Philip*, 1959

Index

INDEX